THE NEXT YOU

The Next You

HOW TO CRUSH YOUR INSECURITIES
AND UNVEIL YOUR TRUE SELF

Stefany Banda

LIONCREST
PUBLISHING

THE NEXT YOU

How to Crush Your Insecurities and Unveil Your True Self

ISBN   978-1-5445-0679-1 *Hardcover*
       978-1-5445-0680-7 *Paperback*
       978-1-5445-0678-4 *Ebook*

To my eight-year-old self who wanted to be an author when she grew up, this is for you.

Contents

Acknowledgments

I have to start off by thanking my fiancé, Nick—who will be my husband come May 9, 2020! Since we've been together, you have made me feel more complete, more alive, and more *me* than I have ever felt before. Thank you for always choosing me, supporting me, and reminding me of my purpose on days when I need it. Thank you for being my live-in motivational speaker, my co-worker, my cheerleader and, above all, my best friend. I love you and I can't wait to marry you!

To my parents—no words can ever be strong enough to express my gratitude for your unconditional love and support from the very beginning. Thank you for the wings you have given me, and the lessons you have taught me that have helped me soar. Thank you for always telling me to dream bigger. Everything I am today and everything that I will become is all because of you. You are my rocks, you are my home—you are my everything.

To my big sister, Jamie—thank you for being my number one fan. Through all of my crazy dreams, you have done nothing but build me up and cheer me on. Thank you for always answering the phone, always giving me your honest opinion and always making me feel capable of my biggest, mountain-moving dreams.

To my big brother, Devon—thank you for teaching me what passion truly means. Through your example, I have learned what discipline, drive, and hard work truly mean. You are always the hardest worker in the room, and I am so proud to be your little sister.

Introduction

Before I started writing this book, it was all just a crazy dream locked in my heart that I didn't quite know how to get out. Then, I heard a quote that stuck with me.

"Write what you need to hear."

It's what gave me the courage and push to write this book. Girl, trust me, this book is as much for me as it is for you, too—and that's why I wrote it. I'm not going to lie to you—I don't have it all figured out. I'm not an expert, a motivational speaker, or a super successful six-figure entrepreneur. I'm none of those things. Heck, I still burn dinner at least once a week and can't figure out how to keep a plant alive for more than three days. But what I *am* is a dreamer. And chances are, if you opened up this book, you are, too.

Being a dreamer is exhausting at times, isn't it? It's kind of like having wings but not knowing how to use them. We're pretty sure we can fly, but we don't exactly know how to. We don't know when to. So, we spend a good chunk of our lives on the ground, where it's safe and comfortable. We see other people soaring and it frustrates us. We don't know how they do it. We realize, deep down, that we have what it takes inside of us, but we just don't know how to get it out. So, we play it safe and we stay stuck.

That's how growing up was for me. I felt this fire inside of me that always wanted *more*, but I didn't know how to do it. I knew I wasn't made for an ordinary, average life. I wanted to make an impact. I wanted to live this passion-packed life that I envisioned for myself, but I didn't know where to start. Instead, I played it safe. I grew up and lived my life the way I thought I was "supposed" to. I got good grades in high school, was on the dance team, and was student council president. I graduated from a Big Ten university, where I joined a sorority, became recruitment chair, and got my degree in exactly four years. After graduation, I went straight into the "real world" where I got an entry-level nine-to-five job with a salary and a 401(k). By twenty-two, I checked off all the "life boxes" I *thought* I was required to check. By doing this, I thought I would be instantly happy, successful, fulfilled, and living "the dream"—but then, one day, I realized the life I was living had absolutely *nothing* to do with my dream.

Girl, I see you nodding your head. Sounds familiar, doesn't it? In fact, you are probably feeling that "stuck" feeling at this exact moment. Your wings are on. You know they're there. But you just can't get off of the damn ground. It makes you frustrated and I get it. I've been there and I have days when I feel like I am still there. But here's what I have learned: to get unstuck, you have to make changes. I know, it's not rocket science but that doesn't mean it's easy. Change may suck, but it's nothing compared to being stuck somewhere you don't belong. Now, I may not know your name or really anything about you at all. However, if you opened this book, I do know one thing—you don't belong in this stuck, unfulfilled, and passionless place that you constantly want to escape from. It's time to make changes. And that's what this book is for.

Today is the day. You chose to open this book on this day for a reason. Today marks the start of you getting unstuck. Today marks the day that you are reminded of your purpose. Before we go on, I know what you may be thinking:

"*Reminded?* I feel like I don't have a purpose. I need to *find* my purpose."

Many of us think our purpose is something we need to find. We do things like travel the world, quit our jobs, go to personal development conferences, or take up yoga. We do all of these soul-searching things in hopes of stumbling across our purpose somewhere along the way, but that's not how it works. I believe your purpose is not something you find or stumble across, it's something you've always had.

We often wait for the moment that our life purpose will just hit us smack dab in the face. Yet that "aha" moment we all hope for isn't going to hit you when you're pondering life in the shower or when you're watching the sunset on a beach. That's how it is in the movies, but, girl, this ain't no movie—this is your life.

Now I don't want you to think that you came out of the womb with one purpose and one purpose only. That's not the case either—your purpose has been created throughout your entire life. As you evolve and grow, so does your purpose.

By the time I actually entered the real world, I changed what I wanted to be "when I grew up" about a thousand times. In elementary school, I wanted to be an author. In middle school, I wanted to be a teacher. In high school, I wanted to be a journalist, which then led me to earning my college degree in journalism. Through all of the career path changes I went through, there was one thing, one *purpose* that remained consistent through them all—and that was to inspire.

A teacher, an author, and a journalist are all very different careers, but they all inspire someone. Part of a teacher's job is to inspire their students. Part of an author's job is to inspire their readers, and the same goes for a journalist. My purpose was always there, it just came in different shapes and sizes throughout my life.

As we go through life, and all of its ups and downs and twists and turns, we get distracted. We develop insecurities, doubts, and come up with these crazy excuses that push us further and further away from our purpose and the life we always pictured for ourselves. I let my excuses and insecurities get the best of me, which is why at the age of twenty-two I was already feeling burnt out, unfulfilled, and disappointed with the life I was living. Once I got my degree, I landed a corporate nine-to-five job working for someone *else's* dream. From day one, everything about it felt wrong. It wasn't the version of me that I wanted to become. I wasn't inspiring anyone. I was ignoring my purpose.

Today, my purpose is at the forefront of every single thing that I do. When my alarm clock goes off in the morning, I am immediately reminded of my purpose. I wake up grateful for the fact that at the age of twenty-seven, my purpose is clearer than ever. Every single day, I get to help and inspire women to become the version of themselves they always wanted to be. An added bonus is that I found someone to spend the rest of my life with who shares my exact same purpose. My fiancé, Nick, built a nutritional supplement company, Bare Performance Nutrition, from the ground up to inspire and help people become the healthiest, strongest version of themselves. Our shared purpose has given us the ambition to create a life that we love. Whether it's through our products, YouTube videos, social media content, or live events—we get to live every single day with our purpose pouring out of our hearts to inspire others. But none of this would have been possible if I didn't decide to finally get out of my own way. It wasn't easy. We *all* do it. We all have times when we get in our own way. But today is the day you start to get out of your own way.

So, what is it that you want? Maybe you want to wake up every day not dreading going to work. Maybe you want to start your own business, or switch your career path altogether. Girl, I've been there and this book is for you.

Maybe you want to be confident. You want to wake up, look in the mirror, and love what you see. Maybe you want to be excited to go on vacation instead of dreading it because the thought of being in a bikini makes you feel sick. Maybe you just want to feel comfortable in your own skin. Girl, I've been there and this book is for you.

Maybe you just finally want to live your life for *you*. You're tired of holding yourself back and making yourself smaller so everyone else in your life is comfortable and happy. Girl, I've been there and this book is for you.

I know what it feels like to have the next version of you locked inside of your heart—it's defeating. You just want her to be brave and show up already. But she won't show up until *you* do the work. Until *you* step over the excuses and make the changes. That's exactly what this book is about. It's all of the insecurities that caused me to stay stuck for so long—probably the same insecurities that are leaving you with that stuck feeling at this very moment. I'm going to show you how I overcame those insecurities, and how you can too. I want you to be done wishing you were pretty enough. I want you to be done walking through life worrying about what other people think of you, or fearing that you might fail. You have *one* life. I'm not going to let you spend it that way.

One of the incredible things about being a human, and being a woman, is that we all go through the same things. For some reason we just don't talk about it—that ends now. In this book, I throw a lot at you. Stories I'm proud of, and stories that I am definitely not proud of. I tell them though to show you that we are all the same. And hell, if I can do it, so can you.

Getting unstuck and stepping into the "me" that I always wanted to be was not easy—and there are days when it still isn't easy. But today, as I sit here at my kitchen counter at 10 a.m. on a Tuesday, drinking my third cup of coffee, wearing no bra and pouring my heart and soul into this intro for you, I can finally say that I am the version of me that I always wanted to be. I'm not going to tell you that I wake up every single day excited, confident, and fulfilled—let's be real here, I'm human. But I will tell you, that on *most* days, that's true. Now, it's your turn. Are you ready? Let's do this.

CHAPTER 1

The Insecurity: "I'm Not Ready"

Have you ever cried in a public restaurant? Actually, let me rephrase that. Have you ever sobbed your brains out in a public restaurant? I'm not talking about in an Applebee's or a family restaurant where you may have done so as a four-year-old. I'm talking about as a full-grown adult, losing your shit at one of the most popular, trendy restaurants in the heart of Nashville. No? Just me? Okay, cool.

If you've ever been to Nashville, you've probably eaten at Bartaco. If you haven't, it's probably because you didn't feel like waiting three hours for a table on a Tuesday afternoon. It's a tourist hot spot for the best tacos and margaritas, and the occasional Nashville celebrity spotting. That being said, it isn't the most *ideal* location to have a good ol' ugly cry session in. But don't worry, I did!

Let me give you a little bit of context, so you don't think you're about to take life advice from an emotionally unstable person. I grew up and lived in Michigan for the first twenty-four years of my life—until I decided to take the leap, leave home, and move to Nashville for a new chapter. I didn't know a single person there, had never lived alone before, and was scared beyond belief. Still, I knew that it was time to put my fears aside, so my mom and I drove nine hours from my small Metro Detroit suburb to Nashville. We unpacked my life into a tiny studio apartment and voilá...my new chapter had begun.

Now, back to sobbing at Bartaco. It was Sunday night, and my mom and I had stopped for dinner before I dropped her off at the airport to fly back home. We were nonstop busy the entire weekend. I didn't really have time to soak in the fact that I wasn't just on vacation—this was my new home. I knew it would hit me at some point, but I didn't think it would happen at dinner over chips and guacamole.

I somehow managed to get out my margarita order to our waitress, but the second she walked away...the full-on ugly cry made its debut. My mom looked at me like she knew this was coming.

"I just don't feel ready," I cried. "I don't feel ready for you to leave me, and I really don't feel ready to live in a state where I don't know a single person!"

My mom tried to comfort me, assuring me that I was ready, but lord knows that didn't help. I remember trying to hide my ugly cry face behind a menu, while trying to blot my running mascara with a napkin. It felt like the tears just wouldn't turn off. Then out of nowhere, country singer Jessie James Decker and her husband Eric Decker walked into Bartaco and sat at a booth right next to us. I don't know why, but something in that very moment changed my perspective.

This was *why* I moved to Nashville. Not to sit next to celebrities at dinner but for the excitement and unknown possibilities of what could happen if I broke out of my comfort zone. Don't get me wrong, I love where I grew up—Michigan is a beautiful place. It is, and always will be, where I call home. It's my safe place. While those might seem like good reasons to *stay* somewhere, they were also the reasons why I decided to *leave*.

Like I mentioned in the introduction, I have a feeling that, if you picked up this book, you are a dreamer. You have gigantic, scary, mountain-moving dreams and expectations for your life. I hate to break it to you, but if you want those dreams to become a reality...there is one place you have to stay far, far away from—and that is your comfort zone.

Cliché, I know. But it's true. I want you to try something.

Picture your comfort zone. Who's there? What does it look like? What does it feel like? What does it *smell* like? I'm serious—get that specific.

My comfort zone is at home. More specifically, my family's lake house in northern Michigan. It sits back in the woods on a beautiful private lake. It smells like a combination of fresh-cut grass, sunscreen, sangria, and bonfire smoke. I'm surrounded by family and friends. Life feels simple, slow, and worry-free—kind of like a cheesy country song. There are no challenges or conflicts—no mountains to move. It's easy.

Now, picture leaving that comfort zone or happy place. How do you feel? Sad, scared, anxious, overwhelmed, and awkward are probably a few words that come to mind. You probably don't feel ready, and I don't blame you for that. Who would choose to leave a place so comfortable and familiar? No one! I'm going to let you in on a little secret, though—the ones who do make the brave choice to leave their comfort zone are the same ones who make their dreams a living, breathing reality.

In my particular case, staying at home in Michigan wasn't necessarily holding me back or hurting me. However, when it came to my dreams, I felt limited. I wasn't growing as much or at the pace I wanted to. I was stuck in my old ways—and old ways won't open new doors.

Maybe your comfort zone isn't home. It could be your current job position that is secure but stagnant. Maybe your comfort zone is Netflix and the couch, instead of the gym. Your comfort zone could be being alone at home, instead of at a crowded bar or concert. Your comfort zone doesn't have to be a physical place. It can also be a state of mind. It can be your habits or daily routine. It's a state in which everything feels comfortable, familiar, and in control. Sounds great, right? Wrong!

Before I dive in and convince you that you *are* ready to leave your comfort zone, I want to set one thing straight. There is *nothing* wrong with spending some time there. At times, it's what we truly need. That's okay—but don't take your shoes off, pour yourself a glass of wine, and get too comfortable. A comfort zone is a beautiful place, but nothing ever grows there. And trust me, you have a *lot* of growing to do.

"I'm not ready" is an insecurity that develops within us when we are too afraid to see what's on the other side. We can say it in relation to a job, a relationship, a move, or even just a new workout class. It's human nature to fear the unknown. However, it is possible to overcome that fear—by shifting it to excitement. I know that sounds strange, but hear me out for a second.

I first heard about this approach from a mentor and it

blew my mind. Think about how you feel when you are experiencing fear or anxiety—your heart rate increases, your palms get sweaty, and your stomach fills with butterflies. It's kind of like that Eminem song, "Lose Yourself"—hopefully without that whole vomit-on-your-sweater part. Now, think about how you feel when you are experiencing excitement—your heart rate increases, your palms get sweaty, and your stomach fills with butterflies. That's right—both fear and excitement produce the *exact* same responses in our body. The difference between the two is based on your interpretation.

Let's use riding a roller coaster as an example. Waiting in line for a roller coaster, you'll find there are two types of people. You have the adrenaline junkies fighting for the front row, and then you have the terrified people who don't even want to be there in the first place. Physically, both types of people feel the exact same way. They both feel jittery—their hearts are pounding and their adrenaline is pumping. The only difference is their way of *thinking*, which we, as humans, have the power to control and ultimately change.

I'm not going to sugarcoat it—this is *not* easy. Trying to convince your mind to shift its way of thinking takes a lot of practice. Moving to a city where I didn't know a single person felt like the scariest thing in the world to me. Instead of feeling fear and focusing on the negative, though, I tried my best to shift that fear to excitement and focus on the positive. If I had let all of my fears defeat me, I would have never made it to Nashville. And if I had never made it to Nashville, I would have never experienced the tremendous personal growth that I did. I also would have never met my fiancé, Nick—which means I would have never moved to Austin. And if I had never made the move to Austin...well, you get the idea. One brave "yes" can lead to so much possibility and opportunity.

Long story short, if I had never said "yes" to myself and moved to Nashville, I would not be sitting here, writing this book to inspire *you* to go after *your* monster dreams. It sounds pretty far-fetched and dramatic, but it just proves that all it takes is one decision. The whole course of your life can change because you decided, in that one little brave moment, to choose excitement instead of fear— and to make the jump *before* you felt "ready."

If you are usually a rule follower, or someone who isn't excited by the idea of taking risks, acting before you are ready can feel overwhelmingly wrong and even stupid. This is normal! I'm a Type A kind of gal. I want—actually I need—to have everything figured out prior to acting. That's how I had always done things. But, like I said before, old ways won't open new doors—and I *needed* a new door. So, I put my Type A tendencies aside, and somehow convinced myself that what I had in that very moment was enough.

Was I financially stable enough to live on my own in a city like Nashville? Nope. Did I feel qualified for my new job? Nope. Did I feel brave enough to live by myself and have no one else to rely on? Hell, no! I was twenty-four years old—no one at that age confidently answers "yes" to any of those questions. I may have not known if I could make rent every month, but I did know that the fire inside of me was tired of being ignored. For me, that was enough.

Does this sound familiar? I bet it does. Just for a second, I want you to ignore that little voice inside of you telling you that you are not ready. What is your fire trying to tell you? It may burn gently and quietly, but I promise it's still there. *That's* the voice to be trusted and listened to. Maybe your fire is telling you to start your own business. Maybe it's telling you to get out of your toxic relationship. Maybe it's telling you to ask for the raise or promotion you know you deserve. It could just want you to finally get off the couch and take the workout class you've been putting off. Do you hear it? Good—don't you *dare* ignore it.

Now that you know what your fire is trying to tell you, write it down. I'm serious—even if you aren't a writer or a fan of journaling. I don't care if you write it down on this very page, just get it out of your heart and onto paper as soon as you can. That's what I did and it worked. I visited Nashville for the first time in 2015 with a group of my college girlfriends. We laughed, we sang, we danced, we drank, we ate barbecue—we did all of the Nashville things. While all of that was great, there was something about the energy of the city that had a crazy magnetic pull on me. This was the energy that I was missing in my life. This was the energy that I *knew* would force me to stop resisting the change that would drive me forward. So, I got home and I wrote it down. Since I want you to believe me, and understand the power of writing it down, here's the word-for-word journal entry I wrote on May 27, 2015—just three days after I got back from my first trip to Nashville. Side note: yes, I know I talk to my journal like she's a person and I know it's kind of weird. #NoShame

"Well hello! It's been a while, but my feet are finally on the ground (literally and figuratively)...or at least until tomorrow! May has been the month of adventure and traveling for me... and it has truly been life-changing. So far this month I've been to Dallas, Islamorada, Wisconsin, and Nashville...and I leave for California tomorrow. I have fallen in love with traveling and meeting new people in all of these exciting new places. I'm a creature of habit and routine, so I'm shocked at how much I have been loving airports and meeting new people lately. I will say that the one place that I absolutely fell in love with, was Nashville. I have never felt so at home, so happy, so alive, and filled with so much inspiration. The music, the people, the vibe...is everything I want and everything I need at this point in my crazy, confused life. I am confident enough to put this in writing, so mark my words: I will make it to Nashville one

day. Although I am beyond blessed and grateful for the amazing start to my career...I've been applying for jobs in Nashville. Although it's a scary thought to pick up and move your life all by yourself...I know that when the time is right the perfect opportunity will come along, and I will be waking up and chasing my dreams in Music City. There's no other place I'd rather be, and I'm ready to work hard to get there."

Exactly one year, nine months, and three days later, on March 2, 2017, I packed up my Jeep and drove nine hours south to start my new life in Nashville. Pretty crazy, right? That's the power your fire holds. It's a beautiful, honest thing that should never be ignored.

Let's keep it real here for a second—writing your dream down is *no* magic trick. It will give you hope and direction, but it isn't going to give you courage. That's where you come in. Let's talk about what happened during that one year, nine months, and three days after I wrote that journal entry. I was working a nine-to-five advertising agency job that was actually a really cool gig—especially for an entry-level position. I was running the social media for a major pickup truck brand. I got to travel and even work with celebrities like Thomas Rhett, Chris Stapleton, and Miranda Lambert. It was unreal and, at first, I loved it—but after two years in the same position, I was getting bored. I felt stuck. No growth was happening.

After I got home from that girls' trip, I started to apply for jobs in Nashville. I was on an inspiration high and determined to find a job down there. I can't even count the number of phone interviews I went through—and after every single interview, I hung up the phone and chickened out. I would get *so* close, but the second it became a real possibility...I crawled right back into my insecurity cave. I didn't feel ready. I was waiting for the "aha" moment for everything to fall into place—the timing, the salary, the job, and the apartment. I wanted it all to be perfect.

That's what I did—I waited. Then, one day, all of the stars aligned and everything fell perfectly into place—I accepted a job offer and moved to Nashville.

Ha, yeah right! Here's what *really* happened: I waited—and *nothing* happened. Finally, I got really sick and tired of waiting and nothing happening. I got fed up with being stuck, and made a "no more chickening out" rule. I told myself that I would only apply for jobs that I would absolutely accept and, if I got one of them, I would go. No exceptions—it was time to be brave. Once I got brave, that's when the magic happened.

I want to talk about one of the things I wrote down in that journal entry. I wrote, "*When the time is right, the perfect opportunity will come along.*" Some would call that a cliché quote—it's really just an excuse. Here's the thing about "the right time"—it doesn't exist. The right time could knock on your front door, shake your hand, and introduce itself—and you still wouldn't feel like it's truly the right time. I can say this with honesty and proof because, when the opportunity did come along for me to move to Nashville, the *last* thing it felt like was the right time.

Everything about the timing of my move to Nashville felt wrong. I didn't have money saved, and the lease on the house I was renting with my girlfriends wasn't up for months. At that point, I had only visited Nashville twice and didn't see much other than the honky-tonks on Broadway. I was given two weeks to either accept or decline the job offer—which wasn't even enough time for me to get down there, find a place to live, or even see the office and meet the people I would be working with. The salary they offered me was doable, but definitely not comfortable. Everything about it felt rushed, irresponsible, impulsive, and just wrong. Yet there was one little thing that felt right—and that was the feeling in my heart. It was the same feeling I had when I wrote that journal entry back in 2015. Despite the long list of reasons why I shouldn't go for it, I decided to trust the *one* reason why I should. I said "yes" to that feeling in my heart, which meant saying "yes" to my dream.

The decision to move and start a new chapter was so incredibly unlike me. I signed my apartment lease without ever seeing the apartment. I signed my offer letter without ever seeing the office or meeting my new boss or coworkers. There was so much unknown and risk in this new chapter that I had committed to, but I was *done* feeling stagnant and stuck. Yes, it was risky. Yes, it was scary. There was a chance that my entire life could fall apart. On the other hand, what if it all fell *together?* That's what I focused on. That's what got me one step closer to my dream.

It's easy to wait for the perfect day or moment to finally take the leap. The day when you have the right amount of motivation, or the day that your boss is in a good mood. The day you have the money, the day you get validation from your parents, or the day you finally fit into the cute workout outfit. That's not how this works though—you are not meant to live your life sitting around waiting for the green light. Don't wait for the right day, moment, or opportunity. You have to act *now.*

Here's my final challenge for you when it comes to this insecurity of not being ready. That workout class you are too afraid to take? Book it for tomorrow morning. That meeting you've been putting off with your boss to talk about the promotion you deserve? Put it on their calendar this week. That blog you've secured the domain name for but never got started? Start working on it tonight. What-ever it is that you have been putting off, I need you to start now. It's not going to feel right and you will not feel ready. I can promise you though that starting before that perfect moment is going to be crucial to your success—shoot first, aim later. You will find a way to figure it out and navigate the unknown with confidence.

CHAPTER 2

The Insecurity: "I Think I'll Fail"

Do you know how difficult it is to do the splits? Left, right, center; none of it seems humanly possible—but then there's that flexible ten-year-old girl who can knock out all three and make it look like a piece of cake. I was most definitely not that ten-year-old girl.

I bring up the splits because it has to do with the very first failure that I remember experiencing as a young girl. I was never the most athletic kid, but one thing I was good at was dancing. I loved to dance with every ounce of my being. I remember leaping and twirling down the aisles of the grocery store when I was a little girl; I could never get enough of it. I always danced for fun and never took it too seriously—until the day that the owner of my dance studio, Miss Diane, approached my mom and asked her if I was interested in trying out for the studio's competitive team. For those of you that don't know, in the dance world, that's a big deal. That means you're good. At the time, I was only ten years old, and while I always dreamed of dancing competitively—I never actually tried out because I couldn't do the splits, which was a requirement to make the team.

I remember being confused because Miss Diane was well aware of the fact that I couldn't do the splits, but she still pushed me to try out. Her encouragement gave me some confidence, so I decided to give it a shot. I remember the weeks leading up to tryouts, stretching for hours a day so I could get at least one of the splits. By the time tryouts rolled around, I had somehow managed to stretch myself into mastering the left split, but the right and center splits still seemed impossible. When the moment came in tryouts to demonstrate your splits, you had to do it one at a time by yourself in front of everyone, which was just dreadful. But I did it. I just kept reminding myself, "She wanted me here. She told me to try out. She wouldn't tell me to try out if I wasn't going to make the team!" But that wasn't the case. I didn't make the team.

That was the first time that I ever really remember feeling like I failed. I didn't feel good enough. I felt sad, embarrassed, and ashamed. I also felt frustrated—why the *heck* would Miss Diane tell me to try out if she knew

I didn't meet all of the requirements? That wasn't fair. My coaches and family comforted me with the cliché, "There's always next year!" but I knew right away that I would never step foot in tryouts again. Failure and criticism were two feelings I did not like feeling, so why would I put myself in that position again?

Despite being humiliated and rejected at tryouts, I still loved to dance so I decided to keep working hard to be the best in my noncompetitive class. I continued to dance (and hold a grudge against Miss Diane) for the next year with no plans of trying out again. Before I knew it, it was a year later and competitive tryouts had rolled around again along with the exact same phone call to my mom from Miss Diane. I was the most pissed eleven-year-old girl you had ever seen.

I refused. How could she? I wasn't going to face that public humiliation all over again. I still hadn't mastered all of the splits, so there was no way I was going to make the team. But somehow, Miss Diane got me and my lonely left split into the tryout room for a second chance. I swear the woman could sell ice to an Eskimo. This time around, not much was different when it came to my tryout, except for one thing: I made the team.

I remember feeling shocked. After tryouts, Miss Diane told me she put me on the team because she saw me improve after rejection. She told me that she wanted girls on the team who knew how to keep working hard after facing failure. She wanted girls who pushed the team to be better even after a bad performance or score. Well, I guess I was that girl. And I grew proud to be that girl, which is why I continued to dance competitively until I graduated high school. I was never the best on my team and I never mastered all of those damn splits; but I did learn an important life lesson along the way at a young age (thanks to Miss Diane), and that lesson was that failure breeds success.

For the people in the back who didn't hear me the first time, failure breeds success. Say it with me now: Failure. Breeds. Success. Got it? Let me explain what this means because not everyone understands this concept, but the ones who do will be much more successful in making their dreams a reality.

Everyone reacts to failure differently, but there are really only two ways you can react. You can let it defeat you and give up, or you can let it motivate you to keep going and work harder. I really wanted to provide you with a fancy example of a once successful person who failed and gave up, but that was hard to find. You know why? Because they gave up. They don't have a Wikipedia page or any notable articles written about them. They aren't guests on any podcasts, nor are they being interviewed by Robin

Roberts on *Good Morning America*. They aren't giving keynote speeches or being photographed on red carpets next to other A-list celebrities. No legacy was left behind, no difference was made, no dream was achieved—all because they let failure talk them into giving up.

On the other hand, I can definitely provide you with an example of a successful person who failed but instead of giving up, they gave failure the middle finger and kept moving forward. That's easy because almost every successful person has faced some type of failure on their way to success. In 1993, Beyoncé was a contestant on the show, *Star Search* and lost. *Freaking* Beyoncé! Before J.K. Rowling became the ninth-best-selling fiction author of all time, she was a divorced single mother on welfare. Oprah, yes *the* Oprah, was fired from one of her first jobs as a television host. Lady Gaga, who has won multiple Grammys and even an Oscar, was dumped by her first record label after just three months. All of these insanely talented women hit what felt like rock bottom and instead of choosing to stay there, they got back up. They didn't take no for an answer. They ignored the people who said that they couldn't do it. They saw the secret opportunities hidden inside their failures and decided to go for it. If these women can do it, I'm telling you right now, you can, too.

In the last chapter, we talked all about fear and how

much power your reaction to fear truly has. The same goes for failure. It's all about perception and how you choose to react to it. One thing that I've learned that has been the ultimate game-changer for me when it comes to accepting failure is shifting my mindset. I used to think of everything as a win or a loss. I either succeeded or failed. But over the past couple of years, instead of losing or failing—I chose to learn.

To explain this a little better, let's get into some of my more present-day situations that might be perceived as "failures," but I now see as learning experiences.

Let's start with college. I wanted to attend Michigan State University for as long as I could remember. It wasn't an easy university to get into, but it also wasn't Harvard or Yale. I was pretty confident that I could get accepted; I had a 3.5 GPA and was very involved in extracurricular activities. I applied to a few other schools but knew that I was meant to be a Spartan.

After submitting my application, I obsessively checked the mailbox every day for weeks. All of my friends were getting their acceptance letters and I was just left with an empty mailbox. I was getting nervous, but I wasn't totally freaking out yet. After what felt like forever, the day finally came and that crisp white envelope with an MSU logo on it appeared in my mailbox. It seemed thinner than my friend's acceptance letters. I had officially started to freak out.

I remember opening the envelope like it was yesterday. I remember feeling the tremendous weight of the reality that this envelope determined what I thought would determine my entire future. My seventeen-year-old shaking hands opened the envelope and read the first word, which was "Congratulations."

PHEW! I did it. I let out my first exhale in what felt like weeks and kept reading. "Congratulations, and welcome! I am delighted to inform you of your admission to Michigan State University for Spring Semester 2011." I reread that sentence about forty-two more times. I'm pretty sure I let out a big, "Wait, what?!"

I applied for the *Fall* 2010 semester. That's when I was supposed to start my first semester of college. That's when everyone else in my graduating class was starting their first semester of college. I remember staring at the letter, wanting to punch Terence Brown in the face. He was the admissions counselor who signed the letter and the person who screwed up my entire life plan. I'm generally bad with names, but damnit Terence Brown, I will never forget yours.

I knew that this outcome was an option and I saw it

happen to a few other graduates in my class, but I never thought it would happen to me. Basically, I was on the back burner of the admissions list. I was good enough but not good enough to start in the fall with the rest of the freshmen. This outcome left me with three options. The first option was to stay home and enroll in a local community college or university for the fall semester and then transfer to MSU in the spring. The second option was to take the fall semester off, get a job and start my first semester in the spring. The third option was to forget my plans of MSU altogether and enroll at another university to start on time in the fall.

Due to my lifelong dream of being a Spartan, you probably think that I would go with either option one or two. Well, my stubborn ways influenced me to choose option number three. It was a mix between a big "F you" to Michigan State and me not wanting to seem like a failure to everyone else by staying home or not starting college when all my friends were. So that's what I did. I half-heartedly enrolled at a different university—and my new life plan was set.

It was towards the end of my senior year in high school and I was (kind of) starting to accept my new plan. But it still didn't feel right. I still felt like a failure. I still felt like I didn't try hard enough, and I was still pissed as hell at Terence Brown. I knew that Michigan State was the school that I was supposed to attend, and I knew that I needed to do something about it.

I got home from school one day and went straight to our "computer room." I opened up Microsoft Word, and starting typing like my hands were on fire. I was typing a letter. A letter to Terence Brown.

I can't really remember exactly what I wrote, but I remember feeling so fiercely empowered writing that letter. I felt like I was in control and back in the driver's seat of my future. When I finally dropped the stamped letter in the mailbox (old school, I know), I felt overwhelmingly vulnerable but somehow, I wasn't afraid of failing this time. The only thing that I was afraid of was the chance that I would miss if I didn't give it one more try.

Fast forward to June, and I still hadn't heard back from Terence. It was "honors" night at my high school, which was a mini-ceremony two nights before graduation. I remember walking across the stage and smiling for the camera as they announced the university that I would be attending in the fall, but the fact that it wasn't Michigan State broke my heart. I still felt like a failure. But the next morning, everything changed.

The morning after honors night, I woke up to a voicemail. It was from the punchable-face man himself, Terence

Brown. He said that he had received my letter and after reading it he decided to call my high school principal. Her name was Mrs. Tepper, and she was basically my version of Mr. Feeny from *Boy Meets World*. She had actually been my principal not only in high school, but in elementary school as well—so she knew me very well. Terence went on to tell me how Mrs. Tepper wasn't surprised one bit that I didn't take no for an answer. I don't know what else was said during that phone call, but whatever was said was convincing enough. Terence complimented me for my perseverance, congratulated me, and told me that I was now admitted for the fall semester. The next day, I confused a lot of people as I walked across the stage at graduation as they announced that I was attending Michigan State University—and not the "plan b" university they announced I was attending just two days before at honors night. Everything finally felt right, and it wasn't because everything "fell into place" or "happened for a reason"—it was because I stopped wishing for a different outcome and I chose to *work* for it instead.

Alright, now let's keep it real because I know what you're probably thinking. "Dang girl, you had more ambition and determination at ten and eighteen years old than I have right now, and I'm in my twenties!"

I feel you. Yes, I was a pretty ambitious little girl growing up. I owe a lot of that to my parents, my older siblings, coaches, and teachers. I had amazing cheerleaders on my life sideline at all times. But if you don't have those cheerleaders in your life right now, that's okay—because that's what I am here for. I may not be able to do all of the splits, but I am a damn good cheerleader.

I had my fiercely brave moments, but I also had my insecure, not-good-enough moments. The funny thing is, as I've gotten older and more experienced in all lanes of life, I have had more of the insecure, not-good-enough moments than the fiercely brave ones. Right now, you're probably nodding your head and thinking, "Me, too!"—and it doesn't make any sense because as we get older, we should be smarter, stronger, more confident, and just all around better. As we get older, we should fail *less*—right? Wrong. So incredibly wrong.

As we get older, failing actually gets way more terrifying—mainly because we have a lot more to lose. When you're ten years old, you aren't worried about forgetting to set your alarm, paying off student loans, making rent, or being accepted by your family. You don't even really know what failure is. You just live your best life, fearlessly.

I became really aware of this reality a few months ago during a ski trip to Colorado. Growing up in Michigan, I've skied my entire life—but you still won't find me on any double black diamonds. I'm more of a blue and green kind of gal when it comes to the mountain. Nick and I were on the chairlift heading up the mountain and I immediately noticed the mass amount of little kids that didn't even look like they were old enough to walk, zooming down the mountain with no poles, no achy joints or muscles and not one ounce of fear. I couldn't believe it! Here I am, pizza-ing down the mountain at the age of twenty-six and still fearing for my life every time I have to get off of the damn chairlift. Not only was I fascinated by these courageous little humans, I was jealous of them! I wanted to be just like that six-year-old boy with the T-Rex spikes on his helmet racing down the mountain. But that's a lot easier said than done, because as adults we are well aware of any and everything that could go wrong. We could fall off the chairlift, we could get hit by another skier, we could break our legs, crack a rib, or hell, we could even fall, hit our head, and die!

Okay, that's a little dramatic—but that's what happens to our brains as we get older. Our brains get filled to the max with experiences, stories, tweets, headlines, realities, and reasons *not* to take the leap because failure is just not worth it. But it *is* worth it.

Here's why: failure is the best teacher. It's true—one of the best ways to learn how to do something the right way, is to do it the *wrong* way first. Girl, I am the queen of this. You should have seen the very first version of my blog, or the number of views I didn't get on my first video. The first version of my cookbook? It was pretty much the "Comic Sans" of all cookbooks. Actually, I would consider my cookbook to be my most recent ~~failure~~ learning experience. Anyone who has actually bought my cookbook would probably disagree, because the product itself is great! It's organized, pretty to look at, and filled with tons of delicious, healthy recipes. So, what part of it failed? None of it, really—but it felt like a failure because of the expectation I had set for myself.

I worked my ass off on that cookbook. I tested recipes for almost a year and changed formats and content an endless number of times. I actually got about halfway done with the cookbook and decided to trash that version and start completely over. I wanted it to be perfect. I didn't have a fancy book deal, or even enough money to self-publish it, so I decided to make it an e-book. I figured this would actually be a better option because it's more accessible, you could download it onto your phone, and you would get the book in your inbox immediately after purchasing instead of waiting a week for it to ship.

My optimistic, go-getter heart was aiming to sell at least 500 copies the first day. Nick helped me create really high-quality video ads for Facebook and Instagram, and I had a whole launch week promotional plan. I basically did all of the things to make sure that this cookbook would sell. Everyone was rooting for me and assuring me that it would be a hit and they would sell like crazy. So just like that, my expectations were set—and they were set high.

Launch day came, and I watched the orders roll in like a hawk. They weren't rolling in as fast as I had anticipated, but I wasn't stressing too much yet because not everyone has the time to buy a cookbook at noon on a Monday. It was right around midnight on launch day and I checked sales one last time. Sixty-seven. I only sold sixty-seven freaking cookbooks.

The next morning, I woke up to texts and phone calls from family and friends asking how many books I sold and what the feedback was like. I didn't want to tell them the truth because I was so embarrassed after not meeting the expectation I had set for myself. Was the cookbook an actual failure? No, it wasn't. I'm still selling copies today. But it was never the success that I wanted or hoped it to be. Everyone told me that I was being too hard on myself. They told me to "be happy with what I have sold" and "be proud of everything I had accomplished"—but that's a lot easier said than done when you are a go-getter and someone who wants to be constantly growing and getting better. I was proud of what I accomplished, but I wasn't satisfied. I knew I needed to stay motivated in order to stay in motion, and that meant shifting my mindset.

It took a serious pep talk from my live-in motivational speaker, aka Nick—to shift my mindset from "I failed" to "I learned," and once I did that, everything changed. Here's my version of that pep talk for you. Are you ready?

YOU get to decide what your failures are. No one else but you. A failure doesn't have to be this catastrophic, earth-shattering moment in your life where you hit rock bottom and have to start completely over. Even if it's something you can literally fail at—like a test, a performance review, or a weight goal, the power is still in your hands. You can choose to see it as a failure, or you can choose to see it as a stepping stone to success.

Over the past couple of years, I have really learned to accept failure. When I fail at something today, I get the exact same adrenaline rush I get before stepping on stage. It's partially because I'm frustrated but also because of the thrill I get from going after something I really want and worked hard for. I am then fueled by my failure and determined to keep going and get it right the next time. I know that sounds crazy, but once you understand how crucial failing is in your success story, you will also learn to accept failure and let it fuel you.

I hate to break it to you, but if you are human, more specifically a female human—your brain is basically wired to be hard on yourself. Because of that, seeing failure as a stepping stone to success is not something that is going to be easy to do at first. But I need you to try. Next time you find yourself feeling like a failure, instead of letting it slow you down and stop you from going after your mountain-moving dreams, I need you to do this instead. Make a list. It can be on paper, in your phone, or even just mentally. Make a list of all the things that you learned along the way. Here was my list that I made after my cookbook ~~failure~~ learning experience:

- I learned how to create an entire cookbook from scratch using Photoshop.
- I learned how to style food.
- I learned how to start, open, and manage an e-commerce business.
- I learned that the internet is filled with places like Pinterest, where there are millions of recipes posted for free...so charging $19.99 for a cookbook and thinking I was going to sell 500 copies in the first day was a little unrealistic.
- I learned the importance of collaborating, rather than solely relying on self-promotion.
- I learned patience.
- I learned time management.
- I learned how scary-low average e-Commerce conversion rates are.
- I learned to not compare my beginning to someone else's middle or end.

- I learned the importance of customer service.
- I learned the power of a customer review.

Isn't it crazy seeing all of the good that can come from something that seemed so incredibly bad? I promise you— this exercise is going to shift your mindset for you. Listen, I know what failure feels like. It's one of the worst feelings you can feel. You feel defeated, rejected, not good enough—you basically feel like someone is constantly punching you in the face. With a chair. But I am here to tell you that it is all part of the process. In fact, it's one of the most *crucial* parts of the process. If you don't look back at your old work or even your old self and want to cringe or wonder what the heck you were thinking, you are not growing. You are not learning. You are not taking the risks to become all that you are meant to be. You are letting failure literally paralyze you. Paralysis by analysis is a real thing—don't let overanalyzing and the "could-haves" and "what-ifs" slow you down. Take a deep breath, focus on the lessons that you have learned, re-strategize, and girl—just keep zooming down that mountain with your T-Rex spiked helmet on.

CHAPTER 3

The Insecurity: "I'm Not Pretty Enough"

"Black leotard, pink tights, and your ballet shoes. Nothing else, or you won't be allowed into the studio." The second my coach finished that sentence, panic rushed through my body as I crossed my arms to hide my stomach. I had been dancing at this studio for over five years at this point, why was this rule being implemented now? I was thirteen years old, aka the age where you officially reach peak body-awkwardness—and now I had to squeeze all of that awkwardness into an itty-bitty leotard. Lovely, just *lovely*.

Growing up as a dancer, you basically grow up in front of the mirror. You were aware of how you looked at all times, and if that wasn't scary enough—you were also aware of how everyone else around you looked at all times. I loved to dance, but I didn't love the constant judging, comparing, and skintight costumes that came along with it. This just goes to show that comparison and body image issues start before we are even old enough to be aware of them. It's inevitable, and it sucks.

Before we go any further, I need you to know how important this chapter is. It's important because we *all* go through this. Out of all of the insecurities I talk about in this book, if you had to pick just one to work *really* hard to overcome, let it be this one. I say that because this is the realest, most challenging, vulnerable insecurity, but it's also the most stupid one. I know that sounds blunt, but I'm serious. It is just downright stupid how hard we are on ourselves when it comes to the way we look. But just because it's stupid doesn't mean it isn't real. It is so very real. This chapter is a monster, but we are going to tackle it together. Now that you understand how important this is, here are some things that I am not going to tell you in this chapter:

1. You are beautiful.
2. You are enough.
3. True beauty lies within.
4. Beauty comes in all shapes and sizes.

While all of those things may be true—that's not what you need to hear right now. That's what we have been told over and over again by society, our moms, our grandmas, our friends, and our partners—but all those statements do is give you temporary confidence. They put a Band-Aid on your insecurities. They don't solve any problems. And today, we are here to solve problems.

If you're like me, sometimes you can't remember what you ate for breakfast today, but you can remember the moment that your sixth-grade crush said you weren't pretty enough like it was yesterday. You might even remember the outfit you were wearing, the way your stomach dropped, and how it changed a little piece of you forever. For me, that moment happened the summer between sixth and seventh grade. Growing up, a part of me always dreaded summer because along with summer, came bikinis—and I hated bikinis. I grew up in a small lake community, so we were always on the water or at a neighborhood pool. I remember always being one of the only girls to keep their cover-up or shorts on until the exact second I jumped in the water. I didn't want anyone to catch even the slightest glimpse of my love handles, untoned belly or jiggly thighs. Looking back now, I was by no means overweight, but I had girlfriends at the age of thirteen with bodies that looked like they should be walking the Victoria Secret Fashion Show. Damn you, genetics.

That summer, I remember getting back home from the pool one day, jumping right onto my parent's computer to sign on to AIM messenger to gossip and recap the day with my best friends that I parted ways with just twenty minutes earlier. This was clearly before texting was born.

At the time, I had a crush on a boy named Vinnie. He was the first boy that I ever really liked—he was funny, outgoing, athletic, and all of the girls loved him. I'm serious—I'm pretty sure his AIM screenname was something along the lines of "DaLadiesMan09" so it was pretty obvious that this guy was well aware of the fact that he was the stud of our middle school.

I was chatting back and forth with one of my best friends who apparently had the inside scoop on Vinnie and who he was crushing on that summer. I asked her if he said anything about any of the girls at the pool earlier that day.

"Vinnie told me that he thought that Morgan looked *so* hot today in her bikini. I'm pretty sure he likes her."

I then asked her if he happened to say anything about me. She told me that he said I looked "just okay" in a bikini. Who knew that just two words could break a thirteen-year-old heart so fast and *so* hard.

It was no surprise that Vinnie liked the thirteen-year-old Victoria Secret model over me. I didn't have a long torso, perky boobs, and perfect long brown hair. Most thirteen-year-old girls didn't, but in that moment all that mattered to me was that the girl he liked did. I wasn't pretty enough.

Now I know that this story is shallow, immature, and maybe even a little comical. I too can laugh at it now, but there's a reason why I remember every little detail of this tiny moment. Insecurity is inside all of us, for different reasons. But when someone validates your insecurity or points out a flaw that you were already aware of, it all of a sudden becomes real and exposed. Other people can see it and it's terrifying. It goes from being just a thought to a reality. Moments like that leave little scars on our hearts and become impossible to forget. And sadly, those same moments shape us into the women we have become today.

I've had a lot of those moments and I know you have, too. I'll never forget the time I was home for the summer after my freshman year of college and my (unfiltered) grandma was visiting—I was unloading the dishwasher and I felt her eyes looking me up and down as I was putting the silverware away. "You've gained some weight this year, haven't you, honey?" I managed to crack some sort of joke about the "freshman fifteen," finished putting the dishes away, and immediately ran up to my room and balled my eyes out. It was another little moment that left a scar on my heart.

Here's the thing about these little moments that we all face—they slowly begin to chip away at our confidence and before we know it there is nothing left. When you are stripped of your confidence, you are stripped of the ability to turn your thoughts and wildest dreams into something real. This is how big of an impact confidence has on our lives. The first step in becoming confident starts with YOU accepting every inch of yourself. I put "you" in big, loud capital letters because that's who has to do it. Not your friends, family, coworkers, partner, or Instagram followers...YOU. If *you* don't accept you, all you are going to do is keep hitting potholes on the way to your dream. Think about it: when you hit a pothole while driving in a car, you might get a flat tire or maybe your tire gets completely blown out. You're stuck. But luckily, that's what spare tires are for. Once the spare is on, you can start to move again, but you still can't go very far or fast. This is similar to what happens in life when you rely on other people or things to give you confidence or self-esteem. Sure, you can move—but you won't get very far.

Throughout my life, I never accepted my own body. I was confident in other areas of my life, but the way I looked was never one of them. Inside, I always felt like I was made for more and destined to do amazing things in life—but I had one thing weighing me down that was preventing me from doing them, and that was the way I looked.

Like most of us, I always had an image of how I wanted to look. I'm serious, I had an actual printed out image of a beautiful model that I cut out of some photoshopped magazine that was taped onto my mirror so I could always have a reminder of what I wanted to look like. I wanted my outside to match how I felt on the inside. The inside me had six-pack abs, a 24/7 glowing tan, long shiny hair, sculpted arms, and perfectly toned legs. I knew she was in there somewhere, I just had to do the work to make it happen.

So, I did the work. And I didn't just do the work, I became a freaking workaholic. I worked overtime chasing after this version of myself that I thought would solve all of my problems. Every little thing in my life that didn't go the way I wanted it to, I blamed on the way I looked. Growing up, I never had a boyfriend. Sure, I dated here and there but never got into a real relationship. In fact, my first boyfriend is now my fiancé! Over the years when I would show up to family functions or weddings without a date or boyfriend, I got really good at using the excuse of being "too picky." But deep down, I always thought the real reason I didn't have a boyfriend was because I needed to lose twenty pounds. I was *damn* sure that the day I finally weighed 120 pounds and had six-pack abs, I would instantly get a boyfriend and live happily ever after. That's how delusional I was.

My body quickly became my worst enemy. I tried all of

the workouts. I tried all of the diets—The South Beach Diet, The Fast Metabolism Diet, The Special K Diet, The Atkins Diet, Weight Watchers—you name it, I tried it. I'm pretty sure at the time I was the only sixteen-year-old going to Weight Watchers meetings. I spent so many of my teenage years trying to find the magic formula to get me to that perfect 120 pounds society told me to be, but nothing worked. Then, college happened and I quickly became even more desperate. I rushed a sorority and was all of a sudden surrounded by nothing but beautiful sorority girls, cafeteria food, and vodka...which left me feeling like any control I once had, was slowly slipping away from me.

First and foremost, I want to put it out there that I will *never* regret joining a sorority. Some of my absolute favorite memories are from living in the Michigan State Chi Omega house with fifty-plus girls. I know it sounds cliché, but it gave me a lot more than "friends that I paid for." It gave me life experience, leadership experience—and not to mention the lifelong friends who will stand by my side on my wedding day and other big life moments down the road. With that being said, there were definitely some challenges that came along with being in a sorority and living in a house with that many young women and that much estrogen. Sure, there was drama—but the most challenging part for me was the constant comparison. I already went into college with insecurities, so sorority life wasn't necessarily the cause of my poor body image—it was a trigger.

For those of you that aren't familiar with the term "trigger" in this sense, it's a strong emotional reaction that is set off by a person, place, thing, or even a feeling that reminds you of a traumatic event, time, or emotion in your life. A trigger can cause you to relive certain memories that you are usually trying to avoid being reminded of. The sucky thing about triggers is that they come out of nowhere and disrupt or derail all of the progress you have made. For me, living in a sorority house—where girls were constantly talking about diets, workouts, and who had the cutest clothes or best boobs, was a trigger.

For someone like me who was extremely prone to body image issues, living in a sorority house wasn't exactly the most ideal environment to live in. During rush week, our job as upperclassmen was to sell our house to the new potential pledges going through recruitment. We would go on and on explaining how fun it was to share each other's clothes and how it was basically like having fifty closets to choose from every night. Well, the part that I failed to mention was how much fun it *wasn't* when you couldn't fit into your friend's leather miniskirt because she was a genetically blessed skinny-minny who could eat Big Macs for breakfast, lunch, and dinner, and never gain a pound. So, every time I tried to squeeze my J-Lo booty into a friend's skirt...I was triggered. Every time I would hear someone talk about the latest diet or workout class they were trying...again, I was triggered. Every time I would see a girl confidently walking around the house in a sports bra flaunting her six-pack abs, yep, you guessed it—*triggered*. To most girls, these were normal conversations and occurrences, but to me, it was just a reminder that I wasn't pretty enough.

Through all of the triggers, I somehow still managed to go out with my girlfriends at least three nights a week, where we binge drank until we decided it was time to go home at 2 a.m. to stuff our faces with pizza and breadsticks. A lot of those nights are blurry, but there's one that isn't.

I don't know exactly what it was about this particular night that pushed me over the edge, or made me do what I did. Maybe it was the vodka-induced vulnerability. Maybe it was my brain being too exhausted from all of the constant comparison, or maybe it was my heart being too broken from never feeling thin or pretty enough. It was an ordinary Saturday night after our usual post-bar pizza and breadsticks. I remember feeling so uncomfortably full—partially from the pizza but mostly with regret. I was so freaking pissed that I let myself eat that many slices of pizza. It's like I had no control over my body and couldn't stop even when I wanted to. So, I decided to take matters into my own hands. I went to the bathroom and after making sure the rest of the stalls were empty...I made myself throw up.

I remember waking up that next morning with my usual hangover and immediately noticed how sore my throat was. I thought maybe I was getting sick but then I quickly remembered exactly what I had done and the guilt started to rush through my veins. Why would I *ever* do something like that? I was so ashamed. I was so embarrassed. I promised myself that I would never do it again. But I did.

I don't remember exactly how many times I did it because it was all such a body-shaming blur. It was usually only after nights like that first night, and I'm thankful and consider myself one of the lucky ones due to the fact that it never got extremely out of hand. But when it comes to binging and purging: doing it "just one time" or "only when I'm drunk" or "only when I ate too much" does *not* make it okay. It doesn't make it *not* an eating disorder. It's a secret that I kept and I know that it's a secret a lot of girls keep because "it's not that serious." But girl, it is.

Here's the thing about sororities: there are no secrets. And the really awesome thing about sororities is that you always have a lot of girls looking out for you. My roommate at the time knew I had a problem and because she is an amazing friend, she decided to call my mom and express her concern. It turns out that being approached by my mom about my problem was all it took for me to snap back to reality, understand what I was doing to my body, and realize that it needed to stop now.

Although the binging and purging came to an end, my insecurities and toxic relationship with my body unfortunately didn't follow suit. I still focused all of my energy on what I was eating and spent almost all of my free time at the gym, just so I could be thin enough. I became really fascinated with counting macros (a fancy term for counting the amount of carbohydrates, fat, and protein you consume on a daily basis) and was convinced that this would be the magic formula for me. After all, it was just science, right? All you have to do to lose weight is eat in caloric deficit, which means eat less than your body burns. If I counted and controlled every little thing I consumed, this had to work.

I counted *everything*. I quickly became a MyFitnessPal-aholic and my food scale became my new bestie. I'm serious, I even brought my food scale on vacation. I weighed, calculated, and tracked every single thing that entered my body from the splash of almond milk in my morning cup of coffee, to the exact number of ounces of broccoli I had on my plate at dinner. I may have gotten a C- in high school math, but I was damn good at it now. I had never felt more in control, and if you're a recovering control freak like I am, it felt good. It felt really good.

Everyone around me was happy for me and proud of me. To them, it looked like I was finally accepting myself and had found a plan that worked for me. I was even teaching some of my friends and coworkers how to count macros and lose weight. But I still wasn't satisfied. I could never lose more than five pounds and I didn't understand why. So, what did I do? Lower my macros, and restrict myself even *more*. I restricted myself so much that I would say no to going out to lunch with my coworkers, or to my favorite Mexican restaurant with my girlfriends because I didn't know exactly how many macros were in the skinny margarita. I turned down my own damn birthday cake because I didn't want to "get off track." And I love me some vanilla frosted confetti cake.

So many of us do this. We live our lives restricting ourselves—not just from food, but from life moments. We tell ourselves that we aren't pretty enough to get the guy, get the job, or go after our dream. So, we hold ourselves hostage until we are pretty or thin enough. Again, we wait for that "aha" moment to give us the approval to actually live our lives. But when you restrict yourself waiting for that moment, you miss out on a million other beautiful little moments. You may not be starving yourself or purging after a meal, but restriction to this level is *absolutely* considered an eating disorder. I lived this way for about four years until I actually did have an "aha" moment, and it wasn't because I finally achieved my perfect physique or hit my goal weight. It was because I decided that it was time for my mind to stop bullying my body. It was like all of the beautiful little moments I had missed over the years flashed before my eyes and all of a sudden, the fog that I had been living in that was filled with insecurity, self-doubt, and hating my body was lifted. I could see clearly—and I didn't want to miss one more beautiful little moment.

Before I tell you what my "aha" moment was, I need you to understand that your moment is going to be different than my moment. But I promise you, you will have your moment. Maybe it's right now, reading this book. Or maybe it's going to be next month at your niece's first birthday party. Maybe it will be while you are driving back from the gym one night, or while you are getting ready for a Tinder date. I wish I could tell you exactly when it's going to happen, but I can't. But just know, it's going to happen. Got it? Okay, good.

My moment involved my then boyfriend, now fiancé— Nick. We started dating and began our relationship living in different states. At the time, I lived in Nashville and Nick lived in Austin. Like I mentioned earlier, I had never had a serious boyfriend or brought anyone home to meet my family prior to Nick. So, when I saw a glimpse of a potential *real* relationship with him...my first instinct was to run. I didn't want my first relationship to be long distance. I was convinced that it would never work. So I fought it, hard. But so did he. He planned all of the trips, scheduled all of the FaceTime dates, sent all of the care packages—he did all of the things. So, I gave it a shot even though I was terrified of sacrificing too much of my "me time," which to me was the time I spent in the gym or meal prepping. Nick was into those things, too (he owns a nutritional supplement company for god's sake), but he always found a way to make *me* the priority. I wasn't used to being the center of someone's attention. I was shook.

The moment itself occurred after returning from a ski trip we took in Whistler. It was the best four days ever—we skied, ate, drank, and lived the après ski, snow-bunny life to the fullest. Throughout those four days, I didn't have a worry in the world. I didn't try to figure out the macros in my burger or spiked hot chocolate. I didn't immediately Google where the nearest gym was or even work out at all. I didn't worry about how fat I looked in my ski suit, or if my hair looked good in my helmet. My focus was on him because I *really* liked him. He distracted me from all of the counting, tracking, measuring, and weighing... and I honestly didn't even realize it until I got back home.

Usually after vacations, I would get major anxiety about stepping back onto the scale after a week off my routine. I would dread all of the damage I would have to undo and all of the extra work I would have to put in after a week of actually enjoying myself. After I returned home from Whistler, I told myself it was time to face the music and stepped on the scale. I was almost positive that I would be up five pounds because we basically ate our body weight in poutine every day. I took a deep breath, stepped on the scale and was shocked. I *lost* weight. I immediately got off the scale and got back on. It had to be broken. But it wasn't. I think I got on and off that scale at least six times before actually believing the number I was seeing. The MyFitnessPal-aholic in me immediately tried to mentally crunch numbers and figure out how this was even scientifically possible—all week long, I ate way more food than I usually do and worked out a total of zero times. And I felt good. I felt rested, happy, content, and somehow lighter, both physically and mentally. And that's when it hit me—this was the first time in *years* that I gave myself a break. I let my body completely off the hook—kind of like when you were little and your mom goes out of town and your dad lets you have a slumber party and eat pizza for breakfast. I felt free.

For years, my mind had been such a messy, chaotic place that was filled with rules, fear, and guilt when it came to my body image. Somewhere along the way, I lost all trust in myself. I got sucked into thinking that my body couldn't be trusted on its own and instead, I chose to rely on fad diets, food labels, and fitness gurus on YouTube.

It was time to take off the training wheels. It was time to let myself off the leash. It was time to trust myself again.

The first step in making any big change in your life is to fully commit to that change. Changes made out of love and respect for yourself will last a hell of a lot longer and stick more than changes made out of hate. In the past, the changes and commitments that I made were driven by the fact that I hated my body, or because I thought I wasn't pretty enough. Now, I was committed to change because I wanted my entire life to feel like that weekend in Whistler. For me, that meant apologizing to my body and then committing to never counting or tracking again. I deleted MyFitnessPal off my phone and told Nick to take my phone and throw it into oncoming traffic if he ever saw me on the app again. I'd love to tell you that it was easy, but it wasn't. Breaking a habit and essentially a lifestyle that you lived and breathed for years isn't easy to do for anyone. It was basically my form of an addiction, and an addict's road to recovery is hardly ever smooth. But one thing I had on my side was my determination. When I set my mind on something, I do not back down. I didn't want to enter a relationship with Nick as the obsessive, restrictive, and control-freak version of myself. How was I supposed to love someone else if I couldn't even love myself? It is impossible to give your *everything* to someone if you think you are worth *nothing*. So, I buckled down and I got to work. I call it work because that's what it is. Difficult but life-changing work.

Well, it's true what they say—hard work pays off. Today, I am happier and healthier than I have ever been in my entire life, both physically and mentally. The urge to count, track, or weigh has completely vanished. I step on the scale without fear. I look in the mirror and actually ~~like~~ love what I see (okay, well, most days!). I eat the burger and fries without guilt. I skip a workout and don't lose sleep over it. I finally have my life back.

Some of you may be sitting here reading this, thinking that you will never get to this point. You may be thinking you have better odds of winning the Powerball than you do of ever being comfortable in your own skin. You're still thinking that if you don't lose the twenty pounds, you won't ever be loved. Or you won't ever be respected, get a better job, be able to wear the clothes you love, or ever know what being pretty enough really feels like. Right about now, a lot of self-help books would probably feed you some foofy pep talk that starts with, "You are enough." But by now you know, I'm not here to do that. That will only give you temporary motivation. It won't solve problems. Work solves problems. So, let's get to work.

I'm going to try to make this as easy as possible for you. I am going to literally list the things that I did on my journey to self-love. I'm talking about genuine, authentic self-love. Not the Instagram version, where you post a photo of yourself with no makeup on and hashtag #self-love just for the likes. I'm talking *real* self-love.

TRY YOUR BEST TO ELIMINATE WHAT TRIGGERS YOU.

I said "try your best" because I know that sometimes this isn't 100 percent possible. Maybe your trigger is your always-dieting mom, and well, you can't exactly eliminate your mom. But what you can do is talk to your mom about what you're going through and explain to her the effect she has on you when she constantly talks about the new diet she is on. If she loves you, which she does, she will support you. On the other hand, if your boyfriend is the trigger that makes you feel like you are not pretty enough, in the words of Beyoncé: tell him boy, bye. That is the one person in your life who is REQUIRED to build you up. If he does nothing but tear you down, it's time to kick him to the curb. For me, this step meant eliminating MyFitnessPal from my life. Eliminating this trigger was pretty easy because I could literally delete it off of my phone. Once it was gone, I was no longer accidentally triggered by the little blue icon on my home screen that used to guilt me into tracking the six pita chips I just ate. Out of sight, out of mind.

CLEAN UP WHAT YOU CONSUME.

I'm not talking about food. This was a huge one for me. We've all heard that you are the average of the five people you spend the most time with—and while that's true, in today's age, there's more to it. Even when we aren't physically with people, we are constantly surrounded and influenced by people through social media. Who do you follow? If it's a bunch of models and fitness gurus that post nothing but photos of their perfect bodies or of the breakfast they ate that looked more like a breakfast for a rabbit, you need to unfollow them. *Now.* I'm sure they are great people and putting out a lot of great content but not for someone who struggles with body image. You'll be amazed at how quickly you forget they exist once you unfollow them. Take an audit of who you follow and when you are scrolling down the list, ask yourself this: do they make me feel good about myself? If the answer is no, unfollow them.

PRACTICE ~~GOOD~~ GREAT SELF-CARE.

During this process, you may be trying to obsess *less* about gym time and the food you eat—but you still need to take care of yourself. Self-care looks different for everyone, and for you if that means getting a massage once a month, do that. If it means getting eyelash extensions and a spray tan once a week, that's great! Do it. Even if it means taking a pole-dancing workout class once a week because it makes you feel strong, you do you, girl! Whatever it takes for you to feel your best—do more of that. For me personally, that means penciling in two SoulCycle classes a week. Why? Because it's a workout that I crave. It puts me in a better place mentally, and the physical benefits are just an added bonus. Self-care for me also means always having my nails done. I know I'm not the only one who feels like my whole life is more "together" if I have freshly manicured nails. Ah, the little things.

TRUST YOUR BODY.

This may seem like a no-brainer, but this is a lot harder than it seems. I'm not going to tell you that your new diet approach should be "intuitive eating"—because first of all, there is no new diet approach...you are just going to live your life. And second of all, I hate the term "intuitive eating" because for years I didn't see how that was humanly possible. I never understood my friends who could only eat a couple bites of their burger and be "full." In a jealous and selfish way, it kind of made me angry. *I* wanted to be the girl who only ate half her burger and stopped when she was full, but I wasn't. After years of restricting yourself, learning to trust your body and its own sense of hunger and satisfaction again can be really challenging. Diets are not a one-size-fits-all type of thing. You have to completely reject the diet mentality and focus on what your specific body needs. Your body needs to eat when it's hungry. Not when it's bored, stressed, emotional, or on its period (I sometimes make an exception for that last one). I had to learn to take a second before I raided the fridge or pantry, and ask myself, "How much do I need right now?" or "What exactly do I need right now?" I'm not kidding; sometimes, I would even ask myself those questions out loud. This goes for working out, too. If your body is sore from lifting weights six days in a row, listen to it. It's okay to take a day off if that means your body will feel better. Once you stop following someone else's diet or someone else's workout plan, and start to follow your own—your body will start to respond the way you always wished it would have.

WELCOME JOY INTO YOUR LIFE.

This is the most important step. So, get your highlighter ready, girl. You must make space in your life for joyful distractions. Sticking to your diet or tracking all of your food gives you a sense of *control*, not *joy*. Don't get those two confused. Find the things that bring you joy in life and focus on that. I want you to be so laser-focused on those joyful things, that you don't even think about how pretty or not pretty you think you are. Once you shift your energy from only caring about how you look to the *real* sources of joy in your life...that's when the good stuff is going to happen. You'll get the promotion. You'll book the trip. You'll find the guy. You'll start the business. It's all going to start to happen.

I told you this chapter was a monster, didn't I!? But we did it. We got through it. But I need you to remember one last thing before we move on: you were not put on this earth to spend twenty minutes of your day entering food into MyFitnessPal. You were not put on this earth to isolate yourself and turn down girls' nights, mother-daughter trips, your own birthday cake, or even a crappy first date because you don't feel pretty enough. You were put on this earth to enjoy *every* single one of those beautiful little moments.

CHAPTER 4

The Insecurity: "I Can't Juggle it All"

There's busy. There's really busy. And then there's what I like to call Ryan Seacrest busy. If you don't live underneath a rock, you know who Ryan Seacrest is—because the man is freaking everywhere. I'm serious. I'll turn on the TV on a Sunday night and see him hosting the red carpet of an award show in Hollywood, interviewing celebrities left and right. And then on Monday morning, literally twelve hours later...I'll sit down with my cup of coffee, turn on the TV to tune into my favorite morning talk show, and BOOM. Ryan has somehow time-traveled across the country to New York City, and there he is, without dark circles or bags under his eyes. Oh, and in between his normal across-the-country commutes he somehow finds the time to host *American Idol*, run his own radio show, produce what seems like a million TV shows, run a nonprofit, acts as an active investor in a handful of tech companies, and has even won the Tour de France in 2014. Okay, so I lied about that last one...but honestly, it doesn't seem that far-fetched given all this man juggles on a daily basis. Honestly, I'm exhausted just *writing* about all of the things he does. Where does sleep fit in? Or food? Does the man shower? If he wasn't the actual face of so many things, I would be convinced he had a twin or maybe even a stunt double. But he doesn't. The man just knows how to maximize and prioritize his time.

Here's the thing about time. We all have the exact same amount of it. But somehow it has become the favorite (and easiest) excuse to use when it comes to explaining why we can't do something. We don't have time to exercise. We don't have time to meal prep. We don't have time to clean the house. We don't have time to date. We don't have time to go out with friends. We don't have time to pursue a new hobby or passion. It's too easy to use it as an excuse, which is why so many of us do it. It's become this magical phrase that gives us permission to not do the things we actually want to do. Instead, we claim that we are "too busy"—and leave the things we love, the passions we want to pursue, and the dreams we want to chase for someone else to go after. But guess what? That person has the same twenty-four hours a day that you do.

Let's talk about the word "busy" for a second. In today's

world, busy is the new black. If you aren't busy, you aren't cool. If you aren't busy, it must mean that you have nothing going on in your life. Everyone brags about being busy. It's become our go-to, autopilot response to the question, "Hey, how have you been?" and this is not okay.

Every time you say that you are too busy, you are signaling to your brain that you are at your capacity. That you can't make time for anything else. It's a state of mind that causes feelings of anxiety or overwhelm, and when you feel like that, of course you aren't going to have the courage or confidence to add that one thing you really want to do to your schedule. So, we stay stuck in busy. We stay stuck in the things that do not serve us and do not make us better. But it's what we are used to, so we stay.

In this chapter, you are going to give up the myth of busyness. You're also going to give up the phrase "I don't have time" altogether. You are going to realize that you actually aren't *that* busy, you just aren't prioritizing effectively. If you are reading this book, I know that you want something. You want it *bad*. But if you want it bad enough, you must make sacrifices. Some of these sacrifices might be things that you love, or that you couldn't possibly ever think of giving up. But if you don't make sacrifices for what you truly want, what you want will become the sacrifice. I know it doesn't seem like it, but I promise you that there is space in your life at this very moment for that thing you've always wanted to do. I've said it a thousand times and I'll say it again—if I can do it, you can, too.

I graduated from Michigan State University with a degree in Journalism with hopes of becoming a broadcast journalist. After interning at a local news station for a summer, I quickly realized that the news life was not for me. I'm a morning person but not when your mornings start at 3:30 a.m. No, thank you.

Although I didn't know exactly what I wanted to do, I stayed in journalism because I thought writing was a skill that was useful in a lot of different industries. Some of my best friends were advertising majors and I noticed that they were doing a lot of writing in their classes as well, so when it came to applying for jobs, I sent my resume to a long list of advertising agencies in the Metro Detroit area. Post-graduation, I ended up with a paid internship at an agency that did all of the advertising and social media for Fiat Chrysler Automobiles. I had hopes that it would eventually turn into a full-time, salaried position...until I actually had my first day of work.

It was Monday, May 19, 2014. It was just two weeks after graduation and I was temporarily living back at home until the lease started on a house my two best friends and I were going to rent a few cities over. It was about 6 p.m. and I was just getting home from my very first day in the "real world." I silently walked into my parent's kitchen, kicked off my heels, sat down at the kitchen counter while my mom was cooking dinner...and started to cry.

"I just don't understand," I cried to my mom.

"You don't understand what?" she asked me.

"How am I supposed to sit at a desk, forty-plus hours a week for the next forty years of my life, putting all of my time and effort into a company that I don't even care about? It's not right. It's backwards!"

But like any good mother, she empathized with me and asked, "What do you mean, backwards?"

"I'm young! This is the time in my life when I should be going after *my* dreams and accomplishing the things that I love and believe in, not the dreams a huge company tells me I should have. But right now, I don't have the money to do the things I want to do...or the time, because I'm sitting in a damn cubicle all day! And when I finally do have the time and money, I'll be too old!"

My mom explained to me that this was unfortunately how life worked and that I had to learn to make the best of it. She told me that I would get used to it eventually. But I never did.

I know this is a moment that a lot of us face, especially as twenty-something millennials. When we have these mini-quarter life crises, we are told that we think we're entitled, we're never satisfied, we always want more, and we think that we deserve special treatment. Blah blah blah, I've heard it all. But for us dreamers, that's not true.

However, one of those statements is true: I always do want more. Which is why being restricted to a corporate environment from nine-to-five, working to build someone *else's* dream wasn't going to work for me. My own dreams were too big. I wasn't going to make my dreams happen in that cubicle. I felt it in my heart, I felt it in my bones. Sometimes, literally, in my bones—my neck and back killed after sitting in a roller chair for eight hours!

From there, I faced a mental battle. There was a part of me that knew that I had to "pay my dues" in order to get where I wanted to be. But the other part of me truly believed that this wasn't for me and that maybe not all people are fit for the head-down, hands-on-a-keyboard, exhausted-by-2 p.m. desk life.

On the topic of "paying your dues"—I have to say that I don't completely agree with the concept. I think it can be restricting and self-sabotaging if you let it consume you.

However, I do believe that sometimes in life you have to

do things you don't like to do, to get where you ultimately want to be. But labeling this as "paying your dues" puts a straight-jacket spin on it. Let's be real here: the phrase is about two decades out of date. It basically indicates that the only way you will ever move up or get a promotion is if you put in your time. All of a sudden it just becomes about the amount of years you have under your belt, which are sometimes spent doing nothing but meaningless work rather than valuable or passionate work. Don't let anyone put you in the "paying your dues" box for too long. If you want more, do more. If you don't want more, move on.

As time went on, I became more and more confident that I wouldn't be a lifelong nine-to-fiver and I knew that it was up to me to actually make that a reality. What I *really* wanted to do was inspire and help people. I didn't know exactly how I wanted to do it, but I knew it was what I was meant to do. It was my purpose. I loved being a leader, I loved writing and having a voice, and I loved helping young women just like myself. So, I started a blog, along with a YouTube channel and separate social media accounts that I could use to create and put out content that I wanted to inspire women with. I didn't exactly know what I was doing...but it felt right. Blogging, storytelling, content creating, and connecting with women from all over the world gave me a sense of fulfillment that I had tried so hard to find in my nine-to-five. It felt like torture going to my advertising job eight hours a day because all I could think about was what I really wanted to spend my time doing. Eight hours at my nine-to-five felt more like an eternity, but I could sit at my desk editing a video or writing a blog post for eight hours and it felt like seconds. Time flies when you're having fun! Or as I like to say, time flies when you're pursuing your purpose. I determined my goal, but all I could think about was how I didn't have the time. I thought about how much more I could do if I just had the time. How much better I could be if I just had the time. How many more women I could help and inspire if I just had the *damn* time.

I didn't want to lose that sense of fulfillment that I was craving so badly and got from my "side hustle." It was like a little voice in my heart telling me, "Yes. This is it. This is why you're here. Keep going." So, I kept going. I sat down and looked at my schedule—dissecting how I spent my day down to the minute. I was determined to find holes or ways I could fit more time in to do what I loved and what I felt called to do.

I started to make sacrifices. I attended less happy hours with coworkers, rarely went out to the bars with my girlfriends, and instead spent my nights and weekends filming videos, creating content for my blog, and studying to become a certified personal trainer. At times, I felt like no one understood why I was doing what I was doing. I didn't have a bazillion followers on Instagram or any viral videos, so they didn't get why I was putting so much effort and so many hours into my "side hustle" that wasn't even making me money. But I knew that I had to get into the habit of only spending my time and energy on things that supported the life I was trying to create for myself. If it wasn't going to take me one step closer to my dream, it didn't deserve my time.

For me, this meant eliminating my nightly TV time—which usually consisted of a couple hours of watching my favorite guilty-pleasure shows, like *Grey's Anatomy* or *The Bachelor*. Netflix became nonexistent and so did things like Snapchat, hangovers, sleeping in past 10 a.m., and mindlessly scrolling through Instagram. Did I *want* to eliminate all of those things from my life? Hell, no! I loved melting into the couch with my roommates after a long day at work with a glass of wine in hand, while we watched twenty-five grown women fight over the same man. That is my kind of entertainment! But unfortunately, *The Bachelor* wasn't getting me any closer to my dreams. Sorry Chris Harrison, but I got #goals.

Let me tell you, girl: it's not always easy or exactly fun heading out to Starbucks to write a blog post or study for an exam when the rest of your friends are heading out to the bars. It's not fun trying to explain to people why you're working so hard on something that isn't guaranteed. But here's the thing: they don't have to get it. You don't have to explain it to them. All you need to do is make the time and put in the work.

During the time that I was potentially thinking about moving to Nashville and starting to pursue opportunities there, I was taking a four-week personal development course that was led by one of my older sorority sisters, Holly, who had started her own business and was extremely talented in the motivational speaking/life coaching space. It was called Mindful Motivation. It was an in-person class with other ambitious, go-getter people who had big, mountain-moving dreams but didn't know how to achieve them. Ironically, while I was taking the course, I got the job offer in Nashville. I went into class that Monday evening and told Holly that I got the job but was still unsure if I should make the move. She was well aware of all of the doubts and fears I had about leaving home. She was thrilled when she heard the news but could still sense the hesitation in my heart about making the leap. She told me to think of this opportunity as a "creative hibernation"—a chance to be on my own and focus on the things that I really wanted to pursue. I would be 600 miles away from all of my friends, family, and distractions. I was moving to a state where I didn't know a single person, which meant the one thing I had a lot more of was time.

So, I took the chance on my "creative hibernation"—and

promised myself that I would make missing the family parties, girls' nights, my little cousin's graduation, and other little life moments worth it. That's how insanely big my dreams were. I was willing to make a sacrifice as big and crazy as moving out of state from everything that I ever knew to make more time for me and *my* dreams. It sounds selfish, I know. But this is your time to be selfish, too. Your time belongs to nobody but you.

Maybe your goal isn't to start your own business or grow your personal brand—maybe it's to get fit and be in the best shape of your life. That's an incredible goal, one that I think a lot of us want to achieve—but it's also one that a lot of us put on the back burner because we "don't have time." Listen girl, I get it. When you are juggling a job, bills, relationships, a social life, and everything else in-between, the last thing on your mind is dumbbells or booty bands.

When I lived in Nashville, I taught bootcamp and spin classes at a local fitness studio. I had two types of clients. Ones who showed up, and ones who didn't. The ones who didn't show up, all had the same reason why. Yep, you guessed it: they were too busy. Every week I would get text messages the length of a freaking Harry Potter book explaining how busy their schedule was to justify them missing class. I'm pretty sure that the amount of time it took for them to write the text message was more than enough time to squeeze in a quick workout. Again and again, I saw clients make the excuse. But there was one client who never did, and her name was Jennifer.

Jennifer was a badass full-time working mom with triplets. I'll say it again, just in case you skimmed over that part. She is a mother of triplets. Not one, not two...but three children that are all the exact same age, that she is responsible for keeping alive every single day. If I ever accepted the excuse of "I'm too busy" from a client—trust me, it would be her. But I never had to, because she showed up every single time. To this day, I'm still trying to convince Webster to replace the definition of "superhero" in the dictionary with a picture of Jennifer. No words or a fancy definition is needed...just a picture of Jennifer, with her triplets. Yup, that'll do.

How does she do it? I wondered the exact same thing. I consider myself to be pretty dang good when it comes to time management, but Jennifer takes the cake on this one. Because we don't keep secrets in this book, of course I'm going to tell you how she does it. There's no fancy energy drink or magic pill—there's no secret assistant planning her every move...the girl just knows how to prioritize. She's kind of like the mom-version of Ryan Seacrest.

One thing that Jennifer and I have in common is the level at which we prioritize our health. I think I can safely speak on Jennifer's behalf when I say, if we don't get in some type of workout every single day, even if it's just power-walking the dog...we will go some type of crazy. It's our "me" time—it makes us feel centered, strong, and less stressed, so why wouldn't we prioritize it? For Jennifer, it means getting up at 5 a.m. before the triplets rock her world—and for me, it means squeezing it in after a long, exhausting workday. While working out is something we do for ourselves, we also do it for the people around us. It makes us a better partner, friend, sister, dog mom, daughter, auntie, mother of triplets, coworker...the list goes on and on, but it makes us better, so we do it. We might have to use a little extra undereye concealer to camouflage those dark circles from waking up two hours earlier than usual, but we do it.

It doesn't matter what your dream is, I promise your day has time for it. Maybe you just want to finally get in shape, or you want to open your own calligraphy shop on Etsy. Maybe you want to write a book, or make your side hustle photography business your full-time job. Maybe you want to become the CEO of Lulu-freaking-lemon—yup, there's time for that dream, too. You just have to make the time to put in the work, or it's never going to happen. Your priorities, whether you say so or not, are how you choose to spend the blessed twenty-four hours you've been given a day.

Have you ever heard of a food diary? It's a tactic that a lot of nutritionists use to get a detailed look inside their client's daily diet before they recommend changes that will lead them to their goal. Everything from the creamer you put in your cup of coffee in the morning, to the mini Snickers bar you ate in the break room at work...every single thing you eat, you write it down.

I want you to do the exact same thing but with your time. A time diary. Just for one day—I want you to write down every single thing you do, down to the minute. It's going to seem tedious and kind of "extra"—but trust me, this is important. Every hour on the hour, go back and write down how you spent that previous hour of your day. You have to be honest for this to work. Here's an example of my time diary when I was working my traditional nine-to-five so you know how specific, and I mean *painfully* specific, it needs to be for this to actually work:

7:00 a.m.: Alarm goes off

7:15 a.m.: Three snoozes later, I am finally up!

7:15-7:30 a.m.: Shower

7:30-7:40 a.m.: Head to the kitchen to make coffee and fill up my water bottle

7:40-8:20 a.m.: Get ready for work while listening to *Good Morning America*

8:20-8:40 a.m.: Make breakfast, grab my lunch, gym bag and head out the door

8:40-9:00 a.m.: Drive to work while listening to music

9:00 a.m.-12:00 p.m.: Work

12:00 p.m.-1:00 p.m.: Eat my packed lunch while chatting with coworkers

1:00-5:30 p.m.: Work

5:30 -5:45 p.m.: Mix up my pre-workout and drive to the gym, listening to music

5:45-6:00 p.m.: Arrive at the gym and change in the locker room

6:00-7:00 p.m.: Workout

7:00-7:15 p.m.: Drive home from the gym listening to music

7:15 p.m.-8:15 p.m.: Cook and eat dinner

8:15-10:30 p.m.: Catch up with roommates, scroll Instagram and watch TV

10:30—11:00 p.m.: Shower and get ready for bed

11:00 p.m. -11:30 p.m.: Scroll Instagram in bed before falling asleep

Seems pretty typical for a twenty-something working gal, right? Currently, a lot of you may have a similar time diary to the one above and describe it as jam-packed. There are no holes for dream chasing or a passion project. You are therefore doomed and forced to stay stuck in your roller chair at your nine-to-five until the end of time. Not so fast, friend. I promise, you are not doomed. You will not live your entire life in a roller chair working on someone else's dream. You are going to find the time to work on yours.

Here's how: I want you to go through your time diary and read every single line slowly. Then, ask yourself: Does this habit, activity, or thing I am spending time on support the life I am trying to create for myself? If the answer is yes, leave it there. If the answer is no, I want you to circle it. Again, be honest with yourself or this will not work. Now before we move forward, I want to clarify one thing. I know that the current nine-to-five job that you may dread going to everyday may not seem like it's contributing to your dream, and you are going to want to circle it. But it needs to stay there, for now. I am not here to tell you to wing it, quit your job, and chase your dream anyway. I am here to make sure you make smart, mindful decisions that won't screw up your life. You have rent to pay, groceries to buy, and student loans to pay off, so you need to be patient. Let's focus on circling other things first, and I promise if you make the other small changes first, the big ones will follow.

Hopefully, you've found a few things in your time diary to circle. These are what I like to call "holes" in your day. Let's take a look back at my time diary and the things I had circled that were not contributing to my dream.

7:00 a.m.: Alarm goes off

7:15 a.m.: Three snoozes later, I am finally up!

7:15-7:30 a.m.: Shower

7:30-7:40 a.m.: Head to the kitchen to make coffee and fill up my water bottle

7:40-8:20 a.m.: Get ready for work while listening to *Good Morning America*

8:20-8:40 a.m.: Make breakfast, grab my lunch, gym bag and head out the door

8:40-9:00 a.m.: Drive to work while listening to music

9:00 a.m.-12:00 p.m.: Work

12:00 p.m.-1:00 p.m.: Eat my packed lunch while chatting with coworkers

1:00-5:30 p.m.: Work

5:30-5:45 p.m.: Mix up my pre-workout and drive to the gym, listening to music

5:45-6:00 p.m.: Arrive at the gym and change in the locker room

6:00-7:10 p.m.: Workout

7:00-7:15 p.m.: Drive home from the gym listening to music

7:15 p.m.-8:15 p.m.: Cook and eat dinner

8:15-10:30 p.m.: Catch up with roommates, scroll Instagram and watch TV

10:30-11:00 p.m.: Shower and get ready for bed

11:00 p.m.-11:30 p.m.: Scroll Instagram in bed before falling asleep

I'll be honest, I did not want to circle a lot of these things. I loved to snooze. I loved gossiping at lunch with my coworkers. I loved catching up with my roommates, watching reality TV and scrolling through Instagram to wind down after a long day. I'm not going to sugarcoat it; it sucks to let these things go. That's why so many people never get around to living their dream—they never let these things go. No matter how much they claim to "want it"—they don't. Because if they really did want it, they would make the changes. So how bad do *you* want it? If you are reading this book, I know how much you want this dream.

Some of the holes in my time diary may not make sense, so let me explain. You may be thinking, "How does driving to work prevent you from your dream?"—and wondering why it was circled. This is why I told you to get painfully specific. What do you do while driving? For me, I always listened to music on my fifteen-or-so minute commute. Don't get me wrong, I love music. There is nothing better than blaring Taylor Swift with the windows down on the way to work to get my day started. But like I said before, it's about being honest with yourself. Taylor, I love you girl, and your music is fierce. But belting out the lyrics to "Shake It Off" at the top of my lungs isn't getting me any closer to my dream.

I know what you're thinking, "Stefany, you're crazy. It's just fifteen minutes of music. Chill out."

Listen girl, I get it. It does seem kind of absurd. But if you want it bad enough, it doesn't matter if it's two minutes or fifteen minutes, your time is valuable and you need to make the most of it. Instead of listening to music, listen to a podcast that directly relates to what you are trying to accomplish. Schedule a call with a mentor or listen to an audiobook written by someone who lives a life that you envy. Fill that time with something valuable, something that will make you smarter, sharper, and one inch closer to your goal than you were before you got into the car just fifteen minutes earlier. The point here is to show you that your time is gold, every single minute of it. What do you do when you're waiting in line at the bank? What do you do when you're getting your oil changed, or waiting thirty minutes past your appointment time at the doctor's office? There are so many little moments and holes in our days that we have the opportunity to fill with value. Actually, as I write this, I am currently sitting in a chair at the hair salon with tinfoil in my hair. Yes, it may seem a little over-the-top of me, but habits like these are what separates the dreamers from the doers. The moments are there. We just need to identify them. See what I mean by making every minute count?

Once you have identified all of the holes in your day, go

back and mindfully replace them with activities, habits, and things that are filled with value. Then, look at your diary one more time. Can you get up earlier? Can you stay up later? I'll ask you again: how bad do you really want it? Now let's take a look at my revised and revamped time diary:

6:00 a.m.: Alarm goes off

6:00 a.m.-7:15 a.m.: Make coffee, fill up my water bottle and work on creating blog or video content

7:15-7:30 a.m.: Shower

7:30-8:10 a.m.: Get ready for work while listening to a podcast or audiobook that directly relates to my goal

8:10-8:40 a.m.: Make breakfast, grab my lunch, gym bag and head out the door

8:40-9:00 a.m.: Drive to work while listening to the podcast or audiobook

9:00 a.m.-12:00 p.m.: Work

12:00 p.m.-1:00 p.m.: Eat my packed lunch and work on blog content

1:00-5:30 p.m.: Work

5:30-5:45 p.m.: Mix up my pre-workout and drive to the gym while calling a mentor (or my mom) to talk about new ideas I have

5:45-6:00 p.m.: Arrive at the gym and change in the locker room

6:00-7:00 p.m.: Workout

7:00-7:15 p.m.: Drive home from the gym while listening to a podcast or audiobook

7:15 p.m.-8:15 p.m.: Cook and eat dinner

8:15-8:45 p.m.: Catch up with roommates

8:45-10:30 p.m.: Write blog content, edit videos, send pitch emails, brainstorm new content, etc.

10:30-11:00 p.m.: Shower and get ready for bed

11:00 p.m.-11:30 p.m.: Sleep (or listen to a podcast or audiobook to wind down)

As you can see, there were no catastrophic changes made here. All it takes is a few small changes that are filled with value. If you are consistent and committed, these small changes will make a difference. Maybe your goal isn't to start your own business. Maybe it's to make time for a workout every single day. Look at your time diary—where can you fit it in? It might mean getting up an hour earlier or going straight to the gym from work instead of heading home to sit on the couch. No matter what your goal is, no matter what you say you don't have time for...it all comes down to this: if it is important, you will make the time.

I'm going to give you a little tough love right now and it's only because I genuinely want this for you. It isn't that you don't have the time. It's because you suck at prioritizing. There, I said it. I'm pretty sure there's an unwritten rule out there somewhere in author land that you probably shouldn't tell your own readers that they suck. But I did. And I'm not going to apologize for it—because at one point, I sucked at it too. But eventually, after a lot of practice, I got really freaking good at it—and now that you are almost done with this chapter, you're going to get really freaking good at it, too.

The key here is to not prioritize what's on your schedule but to instead schedule your priorities. In order to do this, you must decide what those priorities are. You must be brave enough to say no to the things that distract or keep you from your goal. The only way to do that is to have a bigger, burning yes inside of you. I know it's in there, you just have to listen to it. Your goal isn't another chore on the list. It isn't just another time slot taken up in your Google calendar. This is who you were made to be. Make the changes. *Make* the time.

CHAPTER 5

The Insecurity: "I'm Disappointing Them"

I have never considered myself a superstitious person. However, I do have this thing with Super Bowl Sunday. Let me explain. I used to love the Super Bowl. I may not always know what teams are playing up until the day of the big game, but I always loved having an excuse to get together with family and friends while we shoved our faces with seven-layer bean dip and critiqued the commercials and whoever was performing at halftime. But lately, the Super Bowl and I haven't exactly had the best track record. Maybe it's a coincidence, maybe it's not, but it's become a day and an occasion that I'd like to avoid altogether.

My Super Bowl superstition started in 2017. The Atlanta Falcons were playing the New England Patriots. The

Patriots won, which left Atlanta Falcons fans all over the country disappointed. But they weren't the only ones who felt loss and disappointment. My family did too—but it was all because of me. It was February 5, 2017, and it happened to be the day that I had decided to officially accept the job offer and make the move to Nashville. Obviously, at that time my family knew that I had gotten the job, but I don't think anyone thought that I actually had the guts to accept it. If I accepted this job offer, it would make me the one and only person in my entire family to move out of state. I had a ton of cousins who were all around the same age as me...and no one ever really fully left the nest. Sure, we went to college and moved out of our parents' homes, but we were always just a max of twenty-five minutes down the road. So, you can imagine why the fact that I was even debating leaving was a big freaking deal. It may have only been a nine-hour drive away, but to them—I might as well have joined the space program and signed up to live the rest of my life doing research on Mars.

Back then, I was living with three of my best girlfriends who were majorly supportive of my decision to head down south. Of course, they didn't want me to leave, but they knew that there was no stopping the go-getter inside of me who wanted to make her dreams a reality. Plus, Nashville definitely isn't the worst place to come visit your best friend. I never really had a fear of disappointing my friends because they just *got* it. We all had our own lives and we knew that'd we stay in touch no matter what. But when it came to my family, the fear of disappointing them was real. Too real. I was honestly convinced that I would throw someone into cardiac arrest with the news. My entire life, my family had been my rock. They were my biggest cheerleaders and the strongest support system I could have ever asked for. What kind of crazy person would want to leave that behind? Oh yeah, that's right, *me*. I'm the crazy person.

Every year, we watched the big game at my aunt and uncle's house. So that day, I drove to my parents' house a few hours early, so I could tell them that I had officially decided to take the job and talk through the details. I remember that drive to my parents' house like it was yesterday. I was constantly running through different scenarios in my mind of how they would react. Would they cry? Would they yell? Would they disown me? I was absolutely terrified of disappointing the people who had given me everything. During that fifteen-minute drive, I think I changed my mind about forty-two times. One minute I was set on moving to Nashville to chase my dreams, and then the next minute I convinced myself that I needed to stay in Michigan for the rest of my life because that's what would make everyone else happy. I just wanted to be the best daughter and sister in the world. But in that moment, I felt like the worst.

To be honest, I don't remember much about the conversation. I kind of blacked out. However, there was one moment that is crystal clear to this day. I wish it wasn't, but it is.

My mom was in the kitchen and I was sitting in the living room with my dad. "So, you're not actually going to take this job and move, right?" he asked me. I remember trying really hard not to throw up as I gave a response.

"I'm going to go. I'm going to do it."

He didn't yell. He didn't cry. He didn't disown me. It was way worse.

He said, "Why do you feel like you have to leave us to be happy?"

With that, my heart shattered into a million little pieces onto my parent's perfectly groomed carpet. I wasn't leaving them to be happy, I had to leave to *grow*. Tears filled my eyes. My biggest fear had become a reality. I was disappointing my parents. Yup, I had officially become the worst daughter ever.

As I mentioned, my parents were the most supportive people in the world. If I wanted to quit my job and become a professional juggling unicyclist, they would have bought me my first unicycle. They were always on my team, in the front row with face paint and pom-poms. So, it's no shock that even though they were heartbroken by my decision, they still chose to support me.

For years, they heard me talk with sparkles in my eyes about the dreams that I had. They knew that I was feeling under-whelmed, unfulfilled, and unhappy with my life. They knew that I was made for more. They knew that I had been itching to get out in the world and unlock my potential. They knew it was time for me to scratch that itch, so they supported me. Sure, they weren't popping champagne and jumping for joy about my new soon-to-be area code, but they supported me.

The last thing that I wanted to do was go face the rest of my family at the Super Bowl party and share the news, but I knew that I had to. I tried to act excited and confident about my new chapter, but I just kept replaying what my dad had said to me in my head over and over again. I remember thinking it wasn't even worth it. How could something so new and exciting make me feel so guilty and depressed? I had their support, so why did I want to instantly take back my decision and never leave my bubble? Why was this *so* difficult?

That is because I, Stefany Avalon Banda, am a people-pleaser. Or as I like to say now...a *recovering* people-pleaser. I'm sure you've heard the term, but here are a few things that we people-pleasers are guilty of:

- We have a hard time saying no to people because we feel guilty or too worried about the other person's feelings.
- "Sorry" is a common word in our vocabulary.
- We find it hard to accept compliments or help.
- We feel guilty when we actually do stand up for ourselves.
- We love to rescue people. At work, in relationships—we find a sense of purpose and validation when we put other people's needs before our own.

Sound familiar? I thought so. Here's the thing about being a people-pleaser—you sometimes lose sight of what you actually want because you are wrapped up in the worry and fear of disappointing others. You're too busy constantly saying yes to everyone else, so you end up saying no to yourself and the things that *you* want...without even being aware of it.

I truly believe that as women, we are more prone to the people-pleasing way of life than most men are—it's just in our genes. We are taught and expected to support, nurture, help, and take care of the people we love. We are the ones staring at the ceiling, wide awake at 3 a.m. because we're worried that we disappointed our boss for being late that morning or disappointed our mother because we couldn't make it to the family dinner last week. You know when people say that they wish they could "sleep like a baby?" Yeah, well I don't want to sleep like a baby—I just want to sleep like my fiancé, Nick. I can't even count to ten before he is fast asleep, dreaming away without a worry in the world. I swear the man could sleep standing up, front row at an AC/DC concert. How do they do that? Meanwhile, I'm over here worrying about the fact that I forgot to leave a tip for our dog groomer two freaking days ago. You know you have a problem when you are scared of disappointing the dog groomer.

When I told everyone that I was leaving home and moving to Nashville, I did this thing that only a people-pleaser would do. Immediately after telling someone about my new plans to flee the nest, I followed it up with this sentence, "But don't worry, I'm only going to live in Nashville for a year, max. Then I'll be back in Michigan!"

I did this every single time I told someone that I was moving to Nashville. It was like word vomit. I knew I probably shouldn't make a promise like that, but it just kind of came out. Did I know how long I would truly be in Nashville for? Hell, no! You can't plan those things. But the people-pleaser in me felt like I needed something that I could use to avoid letting anyone down or disappointing anyone who truly cared about me. I diverted disappointment before I even knew if the person was actually disappointed. This was some self-sabotaging, dream-destroying stuff. I was setting deadlines and limitations on my dreams before I even got started. It wasn't fair to my family and friends, and it wasn't fair to me.

This went on for months. Actually, this went on the entire time I lived in Nashville. It's no secret that I had my challenges and struggling moments in Nashville. I was homesick. I was lonely. I felt like I was disappointing everyone. So, in a way, this imaginary "one year" timeline that I had set for myself in a way comforted me. I pep-talked myself out of those lonely, depressing moments by telling myself and everyone around me that it wasn't permanent, and that I'd be back home soon.

Every time that I would visit home, I would get bombarded with the question, "So when are you coming back?" and to be honest, it frustrated me. Why did I need to come back? Why couldn't everyone just move on with their lives? Oh yeah, because I *told* everyone that I was coming back. Yes, I missed my family and friends like crazy, but I was also really proud of the personal growth I was seeing in my life. I became so wrapped up in the promises and expectations that I had given other people, that my vision became blurry. Not my actual vision but my life vision. I didn't even know what I wanted anymore. Did I really want to move back to Michigan because I wanted to? Or was it just because I wanted to make everyone else happy? I honestly didn't know. My head was spinning.

We are constantly being told to stop caring about what people think of us. It's in songs, books, Pinterest quotes, and podcasts everywhere. We are told over and over again that once we stop caring about what other people think of us, we can basically rule the world. But remember girl, I'm not here to feed you those one-liner, BS life quotes that don't actually provide you with a solution. Here's the thing. It's really freaking hard to cold-turkey stop caring about other people's opinions of you. You can listen to all the podcasts, read all of the motivational books, pin all of the quotes...but at the end of the day, it's really freaking hard.

I do agree with the fact that there is a lot of personal freedom that comes with letting go of the fear of disappointing others. But let's not forget about the fact that worrying about disappointing others is also a sign that you care. That's a positive thing. But it turns into a negative thing when you can't even identify your wants and needs for your *own* life. That's what happened to me. I was so focused on making sure that everyone else in my life was okay, that I didn't even care if I was okay.

If my dad called and told me that my mom was having a hard time or was sad because she missed me, I would book a flight home that month. I remember getting to the point where I always had a flight booked so I could give my family something to look forward to. I never hugged them goodbye at the airport without telling them exactly when I would be home or see them next. When I packed up my entire life and took it to Nashville, it felt like I took everyone's happiness with me, too. No one ever told me to my face that they were disappointed in me—but I just felt it. Sure, it may have been worse in my head, but the feeling wouldn't go away. And when you carry the burden of feeling like you are responsible for everyone else's happiness, it gets heavy, fast.

It got to the point where I ended up feeling guilty whenever *I* felt happiness. Whenever anyone would ask me how my new life and adventure was going, I would always respond with a version of "just okay" or "I'm hanging in there"—to downplay my happiness so they wouldn't feel left behind or forgotten. Don't get me wrong, I definitely had my moments where I *was* just okay, and I *was* just hanging in there; but I never talked about how much I was growing. Or how much I was learning. Or how independent and confident I was becoming. My people-pleasing ways and fear of disappointing others had turned me into a liar. And if you, my friend, are also a people-pleaser—that makes you a liar, too.

You may be thinking you're not a liar because you really don't want to disappoint the ones you love. You feel like you really can't be happy unless they are happy, too. You feel like it's just the way you are and it can't be changed.

Girl, trust me. I get it. I felt that way, too. But think about it this way—if you live your life to meet other people's expectations—you aren't being your true, authentic self. You aren't making the decisions that you want to make. You aren't chasing the dreams that are in your heart. You are not living for *you*. You are living for *them*. Therefore, you are lying to them and you are lying to yourself.

Disappointing people is never going to feel good. You're never going to enjoy doing it. And although it's uncomfortable and sometimes even painful, it is an essential part of your journey to self-growth, authenticity, and fulfillment. Remember those big dreams of yours that I keep talking about? They only happen if you take risks, and the only way you will be able to take risks is if you let go of this fear of disappointing others. It sounds crazy, but you must embrace disappointment and be at peace with it. You are still allowed to pause and feel all of the things—but then you need to remember the path that you are on, realize that this is part of the journey and keep moving forward.

About a year after moving to Nashville, the people-pleaser in me was just about ready to throw in the towel and move back to Michigan. The year had been filled with new friends, new opportunities, and tons of personal growth, but my vision was blurry. You've heard the term "beer goggles," right? It's when you're out at the bar and meet someone that you find super attractive, but as soon as you wake up the next morning and do the good ol' social media creep, you realize that they aren't nearly as attractive as you thought they were last night after three vodka tonics. Well, in Nashville I had my people-pleaser goggles on, which made the pain from disappointing my family and friends far worse than it actually was. I knew they were happy for me. I knew they were proud of me. I knew they supported me. But I still felt like they wanted me home.

Right around the time I was planning to decide on whether or not to move back, I met Nick. At first, I was confident that there was no way our relationship would ever work because there were more than 800 miles between us and there would be even more miles between us if I moved back home to Michigan. But then, things started to change. I felt things for him that I had never thought were possible. Our relationship was slow to start due to all of my overthinking, doubts, and hesitations, but then out of nowhere—my feelings for him skyrocketed. I didn't want to be without him. He made me happy. He motivated me. He *got* me. The *real* me.

I'd be lying if I told you that I wasn't afraid of disappointing my parents by going into a long-distance relationship with someone who could potentially take me even further from them. That was one of the main reasons I resisted so hard against a relationship with Nick. I thought to myself, "It will just complicate things. Nothing good will come from it." Nothing good? Was I serious? This man was making me feel all of the things that I read about in romance novels and saw in those Jennifer Aniston rom-com movies. I didn't think that this level of heart-pounding giddiness was even possible to feel about another human. And I thought *nothing good* would come from it? Yep, I had officially lost my people-pleasing mind.

Thankfully, and despite all of my hesitations, Nick didn't give up. He knew about the dreams I had and he never let me forget about them. He wanted my dreams to come true just as much as I did. Talk about an exceptional life partner.

The time came where our relationship got serious enough to the point where we had to have the "future talk"—and figure out how we would truly make this work long term. He was more than aware of the level at which I cared about my family and he knew that my plan was to end up back in Michigan. He respected that about me and even told me that he wouldn't mind moving to Michigan one day if that meant we could be together. I'll never forget that moment—I couldn't believe how much this man truly loved and cared for me along with the things that were important to me.

Even though nowadays I laugh at the thought of planning

that far into the future, in that moment, I was relieved. I felt like we were on the same page and I was excited to give our future a shot. But our present, on the other hand, left me feeling overwhelmed.

At the time, Nick's nutritional supplement company, Bare Performance Nutrition (BPN) was growing rapidly and needed to hire someone to help with all of the marketing and social media. I don't know if it was ironic, luck, or meant to be, but that was my wheelhouse. He threw out an idea that seemed crazy at the time. It was to quit my job, join forces and work together—growing BPN and starting all of our other crazy someday business-venture ideas we dreamt up over bottles of wine. The idea made me giddy. He knew how exhausted and unfulfilled I was in my current job, and he was giving me the opportunity to work towards my dream, while being a part of his. On paper, the plan seemed perfect. But I had so many questions. So many doubts. So many "what-ifs." What if working together was a disaster? What if we break up? Was he my boss? What about healthcare and benefits? Do I get vacation? How do we even begin to talk about pay? The questions were endless and left my mind feeling cluttered. I didn't know what to do. After all, I was about to uproot and change my entire life plan for a man that I had only been dating for four months. Yes girl, you read that right—*four* months.

The biggest question on my mind was, was he expecting

me to move to Texas? I told Nick a million and ten times that I would *not* move to Texas, ever. It wasn't in my plan and the last thing I wanted to do was to move hundreds of miles further away from my family. I knew that I couldn't take him away from his business in Texas, so that wasn't an option. But I loved him. He was my future. I didn't want to disappoint him, either. So, what did I do? I crafted a master, people-pleasing plan.

In today's world, especially in my field of work—you can basically do your job from anywhere, as long as there is a solid Wi-Fi connection. That being said, my people-pleasing proposal was to split my time between Michigan and Texas. This would allow me to be home with my family and spend longer periods of time with Nick in Austin. Two weeks of the month I'd be working in Michigan, and the other two weeks in Texas. It seemed like the perfect plan that wouldn't leave a single person feeling disappointed. It was a win-win, right? Well, not exactly. But we'll get to that later.

When I told Nick about my plan, he was all for it. Of course, he wanted me to be with him in Texas full time, but he knew that my stubborn ways wouldn't back down and trail off the path of my plan. I'm pretty sure he would have said yes to any plan that involved us staying together—so, that became our new plan. Logistically, I didn't really put much thought into how I was going to manage living in two states, but I thought I would just figure it out.

The plan was set. I made a trip home to talk over the details with my family one last time before putting in my two weeks at my job back in Nashville. It was Friday night and I was having a glass of wine at a bar in the Nashville airport before boarding my flight to Detroit. The man next to me at the bar started a conversation with me, asking what my weekend plans were and where I was going. I told him that I was heading to Detroit, and asked him what his plans were. He was headed to Minneapolis for the Super Bowl.

My heart dropped. The memories of last year's Super Bowl immediately flooded my mind leaving me with a pit in my stomach. You've got to be kidding me. I couldn't believe that I had forgotten that the Super Bowl was that weekend. I guess there was just *so* much going on in my life at the time, that it had slipped my mind. I also couldn't believe that here I was, exactly one year later to the day— about to drop another life bomb on family. Damn you, Super Bowl Sunday. I looked at my phone and saw that I had another ten minutes before boarding. I ordered another glass of wine.

My parents already knew everything about the new plan and they seemed pretty supportive. The only thing was, they hadn't exactly met Nick yet. Sure, they watched his YouTube videos and chatted over FaceTime, but they still had yet to meet the man that their little girl was dropping everything for. Looking back at it now, I actually can't believe how much they supported me given the circumstance. Everything about this new risky plan of mine was so incredibly unlike me. I was never known as a risk-taker, until I moved to Nashville on a whim. But let me tell you, once you take that first risk and it actually works out, you build the courage to take even more risks. So, I took a risk that put all of my eggs in one basket. My career, my heart—even the roof over my head, all in one basket. And that basket was Nick.

Sunday rolled around and it was time to head to the family Super Bowl party (dun, dun dun). I debated faking a bad spell of food poisoning to get out of it, but I knew that the sooner I told everyone else, the sooner it would be over. So, I threw back two shots of tequila and was on my way. Just kidding, but now that I think about it, that would have been a great idea.

Talk about déjà vu. I'm pretty sure I was standing in the exact same spot, shoving my face with the exact same seven-layer-dip as I told my aunts, uncles, and cousins about the new plan. Although not everyone fully understood this new, foreign millennial concept of working remotely—they were excited for me. They saw the way I talked about Nick. They knew he was a good guy. They were thrilled that I was finally in a serious relationship and also excited that I would be spending more time at home. I knew that everyone didn't truly believe that I could pull off this new 50/50 traveling lifestyle, and to be honest, I don't think I fully believed it either. However, there were no signs of disappointment. Phew! Everyone actually seemed happy for me. Well, almost everyone.

You see, I have this uncle—he's a super protective, alpha, ex-military guy. Maybe it's because he had a few beers in him or because he had two daughters of his own, but he made it very apparent that he did not approve of my new plan. We were all standing around the island in the kitchen talking about Nick and he abruptly chimed in.

"You don't even know this guy!"

The tone in which he said it caught me off guard, along with everyone else in the kitchen as well. He then went on and lectured me about how this is a "stupid" decision and that I would end up regretting it. I felt embarrassed and publicly shamed. I honestly don't remember everything he said because I was so focused on taking deep breaths and not letting a single tear fall from my face. Damn you, Super Bowl Sunday.

But in that moment...something changed. My normal,

people-pleasing self probably would have caved and responded with a version of, "You're right." But this time, that wasn't the case. I don't know if it was the year on my own in Nashville or the newfound confidence I had from my relationship with Nick, but I fired back. And it felt *good*.

I told him that this was my life and my decision, and that I didn't really care about his opinion. The kitchen became silent. Like, creepily silent. I remember noticing that my hands were clenched. I took a deep breath and walked to the bathroom. I would not let this man, or anyone else see me cry. Not this year.

I took a second to collect myself and checked my phone. I had a text from Nick asking if I told everyone yet. I remember really wanting him to be there with me in that moment. I told him that everyone handled it well except for my uncle—but I told Nick not to worry, because his opinion didn't matter.

As soon as I typed the words, it hit me. I was so done seeking approval from everyone else in order to live my life. I was done dodging disappointment before anyone actually felt it. I was done making myself smaller so I could make other people comfortable. I knew that if I really wanted my greatest dreams to come true, I had to start living my life for me.

I recently just finished a book called *Dare to Lead* by Brené Brown. I know it may sound odd or unconventional to shout out another book in my book, but this woman is the queen of everything I've talked about in this chapter. In the book, she talks about making a list of people whose opinions really matter to you. Here's the kicker—you're only allowed to make your list on a one-inch by one-inch square of paper. That's how short your list should be. The old, people-pleasing version of me could have never fit my list on that tiny piece of paper. In fact, I probably would have needed a piece of paper the size of a highway billboard to fit everyone that was on my list. But today, all I need is that tiny piece of paper. And my uncle, well, he's not on it.

My list is filled with people who get me. Every single good, bad, and ugly inch of me. They care about my needs. And while sometimes they may not understand or agree with those needs, they show up and support me no matter what. The people who don't get you and choose not to support you do not get to have a say in how you live your life. And they *definitely* don't get a spot on your tiny piece of paper.

I know my uncle is family, and family is important to me. It always will be. I know and appreciate that he was looking out for me. In fact, I don't even think that the concerns he had and the things he said were unreasonable.

Clearly, he cares about me and that's why he felt the need to share his opinion by lashing out. But here's the thing, my uncle doesn't fully *get* me. He hasn't been the one that I've stayed up with until 2 a.m. talking about my dreams with. He hasn't been the one that I call crying when I feel defeated or alone. It's nothing personal, but he just hasn't been that person for me. Therefore, he's not on the list.

Let's talk about the people who are on your list. These are the people you couldn't live without. They deeply care for you, even if you mess up. These are the people who would take a freaking bullet for you. So of course, you don't want to disappoint them. But guess what? It's still impossible to make everyone happy. Even the people on your list. I know you've heard it one thousand times, but now you've heard it 1,001 times. And I want this to be the time that you *actually* believe it and more importantly, accept it.

This may seem unrelated, but hang with me for a second. Have you ever had a toothache? Maybe it's because of a cavity, or maybe a filling or crown broke, but it's the kind of toothache that makes that whole side of your mouth throb in pain. You take some Tylenol, but it still hurts. So, you end up only using the other side of your mouth to chew until its fixed. You adjust your actions so you don't trigger the pain. When you truly believe that you are disappointing someone, it's the exact same thing. You adjust your whole life to avoid situations or people who might trigger that pain. You apologize when it's not needed, you suppress your happiness, and you get tangled up in promises that you don't even want to make, in order to make them happy. But none of these efforts will work long term, just like how you can't chew on one side of your mouth forever. You need to get *rid* of the toothache. You need to get rid of this dream-destroying insecurity of disappointing people. You have to change the root cause, which in this case means shifting a mindset that you've probably had forever—which means that it's not going to shift overnight.

When you start working on it, you're going to feel anxiety, guilt, and other uncomfortable feelings. Just know that it's temporary. You must stick with it. Most importantly, do not put this off. This is urgent, life-or-death kind of stuff. I know it sounds dramatic, but if you don't make the changes now—you're going to die before you ever truly lived. Without ever truly chasing *your* dreams. Don't be the eighty-year-old woman in a rocking chair wishing she could go back and do it all over again. The time is now. Here we go.

BECOME SELF-AWARE.

This is the first step, and the most difficult. Your autopilot reaction of giving people the answer they want to hear is so subconscious and automatic, you may not even recognize when you do it. You have to slow down and really feel what you actually feel. Recognize the times when you are giving into other people's demands rather than your own. Are there certain situations or people where you are more likely to do this? Identify those, and make a mental note to take it slow and be extra self-aware of your words, actions, and responses when you are around them.

REMEMBER THE POWER OF YOUR REACTION.

Your reaction is the one thing you have complete control over. Sometimes what actually happens to us isn't the thing that is harming us—our *reaction* to it does. Once you become more self-aware, you're going to have more control over your reactions, which in return is going to give you more control over your life. Once you slow down, feel what you feel—take a second. Don't rush a reaction or response. What's the response that you would normally give? Is that the response you truly want to give? If it's not, take back control of the situation and give the response that is in your heart. Maybe the response is silence—and that's perfectly okay. As people-pleasers, we sometimes feel the need to have a response to everything, which leads to oversharing and overpromising. It isn't a feeling that can ruin your life—it's what you do in response to that feeling. Always remember the power your response can have.

GET COMFORTABLE WITH BEING UNCOMFORTABLE.

This whole process is going to feel like you're wearing your left shoe on your right foot. It's going to feel awkward, uncomfortable, and not what you are used to. It's going to take some time, but it gets better. As long as you live your life thinking that you are responsible for how someone else feels, you will constantly set yourself up for failure or disappointment. You need to push yourself to act the way *you* want to, even if that means knowing it may disappoint the other person. Do it anyway. And when you feel uncomfortable, anxious, and guilty, which you will, find ways to cope through those emotions and realize that it is not the end of the world and you can handle it. Here's the awesome thing about feeling uncomfortable: it means you're growing. Acknowledge and accept the growing pains. No rain, no flowers—right?

KNOW YOUR GOALS.

This is going to prep you for the action you are going to take in the next step. It is way easier to say no to things when you know what you are saying *yes* to in your own life. Get those dreams out of your head and out of your heart, and onto paper. Don't write it in your phone where it can be deleted. Write it on paper, in pen, where it is permanent. Those dreams are not going anywhere. Whether they are your small, doable dreams—or your scary, mountain-moving ones, write them all down. Put it somewhere safe and revisit your goals every month. Remind yourself of who you really are, what you really want and the work you must put in. Once you have this down, it's time to act.

PRACTICE SAYING NO.

Practice makes perfect, right? Start with small no's. I get that it's hard to go cold turkey and turn your back on everyone all at once. So, start small. You have to identify what's truly important to you and acknowledge what's not. This is why remembering your yes is so important in this process. If you don't know how you want to spend your time, how are you going to know where you don't want to spend your time? I'm not asking you to say no to your sister's wedding because there's a personal growth conference you want to go to that weekend—I'm just asking you to start small. Start with easy, low-risk situations. Here are some examples:

You're at dinner with a friend and she really wants to split the chocolate cake for dessert. Usually you would give in, say yes, and leave the restaurant filled with chocolate cake and regret. But the new you remembers that you've been really crushing your new clean-eating lifestyle and you know that even just one bite would trigger your old bad habits. Remember your yes, and *say no*.

Your college friends are planning a trip to Vegas and the flights and hotel fares are through the roof. Usually, you would give in, say yes, and put the entire trip on your already close-to-maxed-out credit card. But the new you remembers that you barely made rent last month and have student loans to pay off, so every penny matters. Remember your yes, and *say no.*

You're just about to pack up your things and head to your spin class straight from work, but your coworkers are pressuring you to go to happy hour. Usually, you would give in, say yes and skip your spin class. But the new you remembers how amazing and accomplished you feel after a sweat-filled spin class, and how crappy you feel the morning after three glasses of wine. Remember your yes, and *say no.*

Maybe these examples actually don't feel small to you at all, and you can't possibly imagine turning down your coworkers without feeling an immense amount of guilt. That's okay. I was there, too. But you are going to stay there if you don't make the changes. If you change nothing, nothing will change. Yes, you're going to feel some FOMO. Yes, you're going to feel some guilt. Yes, you may disappoint people. But you have one life. One life to make all of those scary, mountain-moving dreams come true. So, stop making the time for *their* dreams and start making the time for *yours.*

CHAPTER 6

The Insecurity: "They're Judging Me"

My sister has blue hair. Not like a dark, almost-black, blue—I mean *blue*. And it's not just one shade of blue—there's light blue, dark blue, teal, and there's even some purple in there, too. Right about now, you're probably picturing my sister being a spunky thirteen-year-old who idolizes Katy Perry and wanted blue hair just like hers, but nope. My sister is a thirty-five-year-old grown woman, with peacock hair. No, she's not in a punk-rock band and she doesn't work at a tattoo parlor. She's a momma, goes to church on Sundays, and pays the mortgage on her house in the suburbs. She just also happens to have blue hair.

I come from a relatively traditional, conservative family—so when my sister Jamie decided to dye her hair blue, let's just say she didn't exactly get a round of high fives. But did it phase her? Nope. I'll admit at first, I wasn't fully on #TeamBlue. I didn't really get it. My sister wasn't this attention-needing, wild child—so why did she feel the need to dye her hair such a crazy color? Well, Jamie is a hairstylist and she's been one since she was twenty years old. It's also the reason we loved using anytime someone asked what made her dye her hair blue. "Oh, it's because she's a hairstylist!" or "It's part of her job!" was the go-to answer to assure the person that it wasn't because she was some rebellious, bad girl. But the truth is, Jamie didn't dye her hair blue because she was a hairstylist. She rocks it because she *likes it.* *cue gasps*

Jamie has had blue hair for about five years now and like I previously mentioned, originally I wasn't the biggest fan of it. I personally wouldn't choose blue for my hair color, so I had a difficult time relating to her. The girl isn't oblivious—she knew that our family didn't love it. She knew she was being judged. But despite all of it, her hair stayed blue. Yes, there were times where we all wished she would just go back to being her natural brunette self. But today, I'm on #TeamBlue.

Let's set the record straight here. Eighteen-year-old Stefany would most definitely not be on #TeamBlue. She was too focused on fitting in. I may have been seen as a leader at school but inside, I was just another follower.

I walked, talked, dressed, and acted like all the other "normal" kids did. I put normal in quotes because there is no such thing. *My* normal was wearing head-to-toe Abercrombie & Fitch, while Jamie's normal was having blue hair. Eighteen-year-old Stefany didn't march to the beat of her own drum; hell, she was scared of it. But today I don't just march to it. I dance to it. And by the end of this chapter, you'll be dancing, too—without a single fear of being judged.

Think of this chapter as the last chapter's sister. The fear of disappointing others and the fear of being judged go hand-in-hand and are very similar, but at the same time different. In the last chapter, it was more about developing the courage to act and be the way you really are. This chapter is about actually believing and accepting the way you really are, even if it makes you different. The last chapter was a lot about *them* and this chapter is all about *you*.

My personal fear of being judged peaked in college. While I wouldn't take back those four years for anything, I found myself frequently feeling out of place. I went from being a high school Little Goody Two-Shoes to a mortified freshman at a Big Ten university who didn't have the slightest clue what flip-cup was. Prior to freshman year, I could count the number of times I had tried alcohol on my two hands—and now I was living in frat star city where the

Bud Light flowed like water and hangovers were more common than the cold. I thought that I knew what I was in for, but oh lordy was I wrong.

I knew going into college that I wanted to rush a sorority. Greek life was huge at Michigan State and I really wanted to be involved and make new friends. I ended up rushing Chi Omega, which at the time was the biggest sorority on campus. It's Greek life tradition that on the night of bid day, you go out with all of your new "sisters" for the very first time. I remember thinking, "Wait, we go out *tonight?* But it's Tuesday and I have an 8 a.m. tomorrow. Can't we all just wait until Friday?" I knew I couldn't be the only one feeling this way, but to be honest, I think I was. Apparently, everyone else knew that "Tuesday Booze-day" was a thing and they were really excited about it. I, on the other hand was well, mortified. But because I was afraid of being judged and labeled as Miss Goody Two-shoes, I went along with it like it was no big deal.

We were told before going out that this was our chance to make a great first impression as a new member. The upperclassmen wanted us to be classy and put-together when we were out at the fraternities. However, they did warn us that because alcohol is so accessible and basically pouring from the frat house ceilings, that every year there were always a handful of new members who drank too much and ruined their first impression. They told us not to be one of "those" girls. I felt like I was in a scene from *Legally Blonde*, being lectured by girls who were just a couple of years older than me. I was intimidated but knew that I was a Goody-Two-Shoes at heart and would never let myself be one of those girls. Ready for a curveball? Well, it turns out that I *did* end up being one of those girls.

I can't tell you much about that first night out as a Chi Omega because well, I don't remember much about it. I remember getting ready, taking photos, and heading to the first frat house where all of the girls crowded around the bar like cattle waiting for vodka. I remember awkwardly sipping on my vodka-lemonade surrounded by all of my new sisters and dozens of frat boys who all looked like they jumped out of a Vineyard Vines catalog. I remember finally loosening up and thinking to myself, "Okay, okay...I can handle this!" and ironically, that's about the last thought I remember.

The next morning as I was opening my eyes, I realized that I was not in my dorm room. I slowly got up from the couch and a piece of sliced bread fell off of my lap. What the heck. I was in my outfit from the night before and my purse was on the coffee table. I looked around and finally realized where I was. I was in one of the corner lounges at the Chi Omega house. I was so confused. I didn't remember anything from the night before. Why wasn't I in my dorm room? How did I get here? And why the hell was I covered in sliced bread?

There was another girl sleeping on the couch across from me. I didn't recognize her, but I figured she must be an upperclassman living in the house. She heard me get up and immediately sprung up and looked relieved to see me alive and breathing.

I told her how I didn't remember a single thing and asked her how I got there. She then went on to tell me that they found me passed out in a chair at a frat house, so they took me back to Chi Omega. I was mortified. I had heard of the term *blacking out,* but I had never actually experienced it. I felt scared. I felt confused. I felt judged.

I noticed the trash can a few feet away from me. Well, now the sliced bread made sense. I didn't even know these girls' names and they were already holding my hair back. I immediately felt the urge to throw up again—not because of the hangover, but because of the humiliation. I was officially one of those girls. Great.

I remember frantically trying to explain myself and convince them that this wasn't who I was and how this had never happened to me before. I'm pretty sure I even pulled out the desperate "I was student council president!" card to show them that I really was a responsible, Goody Two-Shoes and not some loosey-goose blacked-out bimbo. It was the first time that I actually wanted to be called a Goody Two-Shoes. Sure, I had felt judged before but not on this level. If sororities had some kind of secret burn book like they did in the movie *Mean Girls*, I'm absolutely positive that I would be on the cover.

I knew going into the whole sorority recruitment process that I would be judged, but I didn't think that I would be misjudged. These girls didn't know me. They didn't know that what happened that night wasn't a normal occurrence for me or that it really *wasn't* who I was. So why would they believe me? Their opinion of me was their opinion, and it was hard to swallow knowing that I couldn't change it.

After that night, I told myself that I would never let that happen again—and it didn't. Even to this day, I've never blacked out or lost complete control like that again—it's just not something that I like to do or feel. That night shook me and reminded me of who I really wanted to be and what my values were. The only problem was, who I really wanted to be didn't exactly thrive in a Big Ten university environment. College was a struggle for me. I was constantly juggling the pressure to go out drinking every night from Tuesday to Saturday with the way I really wanted to spend my time. If I stayed in to go to the gym, study, or meet a deadline for the college newspaper I wrote for—I felt judged. But when you're nineteen, insecure, and living on your own for the very first time—you'll do anything to fit in. So, in an effort to fit in and avoid all judgment, I put all of the things that I really wanted to do and the person that I really wanted to be on the back burner. And they stayed on the back burner for the next four years.

Is your highlighter out? Get it ready, girl, because this is a biggie. This is something that you need to remember:

> Your dreams, the things you want to accomplish, the person that *you* want to be—should *never* be placed on the back burner of your life.

They don't belong there because you're afraid of what other people will think. If they are doubting you, criticizing you, laughing at you, or judging you—that's a good thing, because that means your dreams are big enough and worth fighting for.

After college graduation, I decided to take my dreams off the back burner, but they still didn't make it to the front. You know that awkward middle burner that gets a little bit more action than the back burner, but still never really gets used? Yeah, that's where my dreams were. I knew that I really wanted to start a YouTube channel and blog so I could help inspire women. I wanted to jump in head-first and give it everything I had, but there was one thing still holding me back. It was a little voice that stopped me from going all in that said, "But what will they think?"

It was right around 2014 when the whole Youtuber and vlogger concept got *really* popular. I saw people across all different types of industries pick up the camera to document their lives and inspire others. I was captivated by it and had a feeling that this could one day be the new version of cable television—so I wanted to jump on board as soon as I possibly could. That Christmas, my sweet mom got me my very first camera and lighting kit. I was so excited to start creating content and put it out into the world. I was on a high and finally felt like I was making some serious moves towards my dreams. But then the voice came back. "But what will they think?"

At the time, I didn't know anyone on a personal level who was trying to do what I was doing, let alone anyone who actually understood it. What if they think my videos are stupid? What if no one watches them? What if they talk behind my back? The list of what-ifs was endless, and they were starting to make me second-guess everything. The voice was loud and I couldn't ignore it.

When it came time to set up the social media channels for my blog and more specifically, Instagram, I debated whether or not to use my personal Instagram to post all of my blog content on. I already had a few hundred followers on my personal Instagram—so it *would* give me a little head start. But just like clockwork, the voice was back. "But what will they think?"

Immediately, I made the decision to make a separate Instagram account. The people who followed my personal Instagram were mostly just my family, friends, and coworkers, and I did not want to deal with that. What if they think I'm annoying? What if they make fun of me? What if they don't take me seriously? I was back at it with the mile-long list of what-ifs and decided that it would be a much safer option to start fresh so I wouldn't have to deal with being judged. This is what a lot of us do when we are afraid of what they'll think—we play it safe. We don't take risks, we do it the way we've always done it, and then we wonder why we're still stuck. But that's *exactly* why we're stuck.

You cannot reach your highest potential by playing it safe. In fact, playing it safe is the biggest risk of all. If you play it safe your entire life because you don't want to be judged, you risk never actually living your life. Remember that eighty-year-old woman in the rocking chair with all of her dreams still locked in her heart? I know that's not what you want, so it's time to stop playing it safe.

I started creating content and putting it out into the world, but it started to feel like I was living a double life. It felt like I was keeping my dream a secret, and something about it didn't feel right. During the time I started to film videos for my YouTube channel, I lived with three of my best friends—and they were the most supportive friends ever. One of them in particular, Katie, was always rooting for me. She was my personal cheerleader in everything I did, and still is to this day. She loved my videos and always encouraged me to keep going. But even with her support and encouragement, I felt embarrassed. I would wait until all of my roommates left the house before I filmed a video because for some reason, I felt insecure about what they would think. I felt like I needed to hide my passion.

Here I was, making videos and writing blog posts on how to stay motivated and be your authentic self, but I wasn't even doing that myself. I felt like a phony. I felt like I was hiding half of my heart and the person I really wanted to be because it was just too different. Just when I would work up the courage and give myself a personal pep talk to stop hiding my dream, something would happen that would invite that little voice back inside my head. Even though I made a separate Instagram, some of my friends, family, and coworkers stumbled across the account and caught on. They would call my blog and videos things like *little* and *cute*. They would leave sarcastic comments on things I posted. I let them make me feel like my dreams were small. The worst part was, I started to believe them.

Like I mentioned in the last chapter, Pinterest quotes, podcasts, books, and motivational speakers are constantly telling us to stop caring what other people think of us. They make it seem like a piece of cake, don't they? Like it's a switch that you can easily turn on and off. It drives me crazy whenever anyone makes it seem easy because it's not. They tell us to "ignore them" or to remember that "you can't please everyone," or my personal favorite, to "not take things so personally." But if you are a real human with real emotions, you know that's a lot easier said than done.

Imagine walking into your doctor's office because you are experiencing some back pain. You tell the doctor all about your pain and symptoms—and it seems like he's really listening and is concerned. Then, after examining your back he responds with, "My suggestion and advice for you is to stop having back pain."

Wait, what? Sounds crazy, right? You were expecting to walk out of there with some type of treatment plan, whether it was medication, a referral to a specialist, or even one of those dumb worksheets with relief exercises on it. But you were supposed to stop having back pain by stopping having back pain? That makes no sense. It seems impossible, doesn't it? Well, that's how I felt every single time someone would tell me to "ignore them."

How do you feel when someone tells you to just brush it off and "ignore them?" If you're like me, it probably pisses you off. In fact, you probably want to punch whoever told you to "ignore them" in the face. Your response is usually something like "I know; you're right!" but deep down, you have no idea how to actually stop fearing being judged. It becomes a vicious cycle—you give yourself a pep talk and tell yourself to stop caring, but then a few hours later you're stressing about the number of likes the photo of you in your bikini didn't get on Instagram.

So why does this happen? Why do we allow other people to have so much control over how we choose to live our lives? Why do we let their opinion determine the car we should be driving, the clothes we should be wearing, the way we style our hair, or the food we eat? It's because we are seeking validation. We are *all* seeking validation. While some people may claim that they really *don't* care what others think of them—I don't believe that's entirely true. Some people just manage to hide it more than others. We all have a self-image of ourselves—a picture in our heads of how we think people perceive us. It's how we hope people perceive us. It's natural to want validation that your self-image is accurate. You want it from your parents, your boss, your boyfriend, your best friend, and sometimes even your followers on social media. You want all of those people to validate your self-image. You want to be approved of. You want to be loved. And it's all because we don't trust ourselves to make our own judgments. All of a sudden, it's not enough to be self-satisfied. We need others to be satisfied, too. This sounds familiar, doesn't it? I've been there. I have days where I am still there.

When someone would poke fun at my blog or motivational videos, I used to want to crawl in a hole and die. It got to the point where I would delete videos that I spent hours shooting and editing because *one* person left a sarcastic or snarky comment. I used to let them make me feel ashamed and embarrassed. I used to let them ruin my day, or even my entire week. I used to let them make me feel like I wasn't enough. I used to let *them* be in the driver's seat of *my* dreams. But here's the thing about people who judge you: it's not about you. It's about them.

It's about their insecurities. It's about what they think of themselves. None of those things have to do with you. They are simply just trying to bring you back down to their level so they feel comfortable again. I want you to think of a time where you felt judged. Or maybe a time where you felt like someone was trying to make your dream feel small by criticizing you. Now I want you to think about that person. What are they doing with their life? Are they doing more than you? Are they doing better than you? No, they aren't. And guess what, girl? The answer will *always* be no. You will never be criticized or judged by someone who is doing more than you. The ones criticizing you are the ones doing *less* than you. Read that again, because I need you to remember it. The ones who are judging you don't understand you. They don't understand the dream that you are chasing. The people who judge you aren't like you. They don't speak the language of your heart or even try to. They might as well be on a different planet. That's how different you are from them. However, the people who do understand will never judge you. If they've been through it, if they've successfully done what you are trying to do—they will do nothing but cheer you on. If you constantly spend time caring about the opinions of people who don't understand you, you will end up staying exactly where they are. And that is not where you belong.

That means that the douchebag at work telling you that your half-marathon time sucked probably has never even run a 5K. That means that the Debby-downer telling you that your business idea will never succeed is probably miserable with their own career. That means that the mean girl staring your outfit up and down with judgy eyes is probably drowning in her own insecurities. When they judge you, it doesn't define who you are—it defines who they are.

For me, that meant taking a look at the people who were constantly giving me unsolicited advice or direction, and asking myself—are they where I want to be? Again, the answer was always no. So instead of taking it personally, I would nod, smile, and let it go in one ear and out the other. There's always going to be someone telling you to do it a different way. There's always going to be someone telling you to not spend *that* much money. There's always going to be someone telling you that it's not going to work. There's always going to be someone who says, "I told you so." Unfortunately, those people will always be there waiting for you to fall and waiting for the day that you won't get back up. Yes, sometimes in life, falling is inevitable. It's a part of the process. It's an accident. But staying down is a choice.

Remember that little voice in my head that would show up whenever I wanted to do something brave? The one saying, "But what will they think?" Well, I'm going to be honest with you: it hasn't fully gone away and it probably never will. But over the past couple of years, I have started to use it to my advantage. It's a mental trick that I use to help shift my thinking. I've used that little (okay, sometimes obnoxious) voice of judgment to remind me how brave I am about to be. I let it remind me that what I'm doing is going to make me grow. I let it remind me that I am getting closer to my goal or dream. It has become a tool that helps me get closer to the *me* I really want to be. So next time that little voice is trying to rock your world and derail your dreams, think of it as a little mental notification that reminds you that what you're doing means something. Let it remind you that you are being your true, authentic self.

Now I know this trick may not seem like it works for every

scenario, but it does. Let me give you an example. Let's say you are finally fed up with the fact that you can't run a mile without feeling like you are going to pass out. You are ready to make your health and fitness a priority and really want to make the changes, but you are terrified of the gym. The grunting buff bros and women taking selfies in their sports bras intimidate you so much that you can't even bring yourself to walk through the front doors. You're scared that they'll judge you for running slow. You're scared that they'll judge you for the way you look in your workout clothes. You're scared that they'll judge you for how red your face gets during a workout. All of these fears literally paralyze you from going after what you want for yourself. You have two options in this scenario. You're always going to have two options. The first option is letting the little voice win, because you are too afraid of what they'll think. You may think the second option is to ignore the voice—but I actually want you to listen to it. Let it remind you that what you are doing is going to make you grow. Let it remind you that if you decide to walk through those doors and take that first step onto that treadmill, you are one step, one day, and one moment closer to your goal or dream. Don't let the voice win. All it takes is one brave moment in saying yes to yourself and bye Felicia to them and their opinions.

I'm going to let you in on one last little secret that is going to help you overcome this insecurity: people don't judge us as much as we think. It actually might be kind of disappointing to realize that people don't care as much as we think. People are way more concerned with their own families, careers, workout routines, diets, and weekend plans than they are about ours. I'm not pointing this out to make you feel better; I'm pointing this out because it's the truth. You know when you are in the beginning of a relationship and you're mortified for the moment that your new boo has to see you without makeup? I know you know what I'm talking about, girl. You know, when you have your very first sleepover and you make sure to wake up before him and tiptoe to the bathroom to put concealer on your dark circles and zit the size of Jupiter that's taken residence on your chin. You're afraid that he'll judge you for your imperfections, so you try your best to cover them up. Then when the day finally does come when he sees you without makeup, he doesn't even say anything. He doesn't even notice Jupiter on your chin. Sure, it may be because he's a guy, but it's also because as women, we are about fifty times more critical of ourselves than men are. Like I said, I know this may not make you feel better, but it's something that I want you to try to remember.

So, here's what I need you to do. I need you to pick one thing that you've been wanting to do for what seems like forever. It doesn't matter what it is, but it has to be something you haven't done yet because you are afraid of what they will think. Maybe you want to take a dance class or enroll in cooking classes. Maybe you want to stay in and work on your blog instead of going out and partying with your friends. Maybe you want to go to a personal development conference, or start your own blog. Girl, maybe all you want to do is dye your hair blue. That's fine. It doesn't matter what it is, you just need to do it. And when that little voice tries to wiggle its way back into your mind, give it the middle finger, tell it to shut up, close your eyes and jump. It's the only way you're going to prove to yourself that it's not about them or what they think. It's about you.

CHAPTER 7

The Insecurity: "I Don't Know How"

Has someone ever told you to "Google it?" Doesn't it kind of just piss you off? That response used to make my blood boil. I would already be frustrated because I didn't know the answer or know how to do it—and as soon as I would ask someone for help and in return was told to just "Google it," I immediately wanted to flip a freaking table. Why couldn't they just *show* me how to do it? I instantly felt dumb. They made it seem so easy. They made it seem like all of the answers to everything on planet earth are just sitting on Google, available for everyone. But then one day, it hit me. All of the answers to everything on planet earth *are* just sitting on Google. For free. Well, shit.

Just a quick heads up—you aren't getting cut any slack during this chapter, sister. Harsh, I know, but this insecurity just doesn't fly in today's world. In my opinion, it isn't even an insecurity; it's an excuse. It might have been a valid excuse a few decades ago but not today. But as humans it's still one of our favorite (and laziest) excuses to fall back on when it comes to well, everything. Especially our dreams. We want to lose weight and grow pretty muscles, but we don't know how. So we don't. We want to start our own blog, but we don't know how, so we don't. We want to build a six-figure business, learn another language, earn our doctorate, write a book, climb Mount Everest—but we don't know how. So our dreams stay put, locked inside our hearts.

I'm going to tell you a story that I am not exactly proud of. It happened in fifth grade, which makes it comical, but a part of me still gets pissed at my ten-year-old self whenever I think about it. I promise I won't get offended if you laugh because this story is absolutely absurd—but there *is* something I want you to take away from it.

In most elementary schools, there is a fifth-grade band. You've moved up in the world and have mastered "Hot Cross Buns" on the recorder and it's finally time to choose a real instrument to learn how to play. So I chose the flute. The flute was the instrument that all of the cool girls played—so of course, picking that as my instrument was a no-brainer. I had taken piano lessons years before, so I thought that I had a pretty good chance of mastering the flute. But I actually ended up having a really hard time. All of the other students playing the flute made it seem like a piece of cake, and then there was me, covered in my own slobber without a single note being hit. However, I was never really too worried—I just figured that I wouldn't sign up for any solos. So I never asked for help. I never told anyone that I couldn't actually play. I just faked it. It was pretty easy to do in a band of one-hundred fifth graders.

Recital season was approaching—and our band teacher, Mr. Chisholm, told the band that we had to be individually tested to determine what chair we would sit in on stage at the recital. Oh *snap*. I couldn't even freaking play "Mary Had a Little Lamb"—how was I supposed to get through this test? I remember losing sleep over the thought of spitting all over Mr. Chisholm's perfectly ironed dress shirt and bow tie. I tried to practice a couple of times, but I just couldn't get it down. So I gave up. When the day of the test finally came, I got desperate.

I had to get out of this test. And while I could have faked sick, lost my flute, or really pulled off any of the other common-sense methods to get out of the test—I chose to *break* the flute. I'm serious. I took the flute and banged it as hard as I possibly could against a metal bench while no one was looking. Again, I don't have any explanation for this, other than me being ten years old and panicked.

Picture me, a sweet little ten-year-old girl dressed head to toe in Limited Too, violently smashing a flute against a bench. Go ahead, you now have my permission to laugh.

I remember showing the flute to Mr. Chisolm and the man had to know something was up. I'm pretty sure I told him that I dropped it, ha! The only damage that was (surprisingly) done to the flute was a dent in the mouth-piece, which did prevent me from playing. He let me off the hook, and part of me thinks it was because he knew the real reason why I didn't want to take the test. So a few weeks later, I got to sit in the back row of the band during the recital while I faked playing every single song from start to finish on a replacement flute.

I didn't tell you this story to inspire you. Let's be real here; I was in fifth grade. I told you this story to show you how important effort is when it comes to achieving a goal. I put in zero effort when it came to the flute. Who knows? Maybe I could have been the next child prodigy flutist if I would have just tried to learn. Well, probably not...but you get what I'm saying. You don't know what you are capable of if you don't even try.

Here's the thing, girl. None of us come into this world as millionaires. None of us come into this world speaking three different languages or as a *New York Times* best-selling author. When we come into this world, we are all equal little eight-pound blobs that don't know anything other than our mother's boob. We're all the same. But what eventually sets us apart from one another is how hard we are willing to work for what we want. The life we want. The people who do become millionaires and do become *New York Times* best-selling authors *work* for it. But part of working for it is learning. If you are not willing to learn, no one can help you. But if you are determined to learn, no one can stop you.

We are all guilty of using "I don't know how" as an excuse. Sometimes, it's because we're feeling lazy and it's the way we get out of doing something that we don't really want to do in the first place. We've all had a husband, fiancé, boyfriend, or brother tell us they can't mow the lawn, mop the floors, or fold the laundry because "they don't know how." *Really?* That's a pathetic (and annoying) example of using the excuse to get out of a boring chore that we don't want to do. But why are we using this excuse to keep us from doing the things in life we actually *do* want to do? Saying "I don't know how" lets you off the hook from ever figuring out how to do something. So why are you letting yourself off the hook from your own dreams?

Let's talk about why this excuse doesn't work in today's world. Decades ago, there was no such thing as Google, YouTube, podcasts, audiobooks, masterminds, or online courses. If you wanted to learn how to do something, you either had to go to school, go to an actual library and open an actual book, or gasp—ask an actual human being, who knew how to do it, for help face-to-face. Nowadays, the world is literally at your fingertips. Want to learn how to change a tire? YouTube has a tutorial for that. Want to learn how to say "hello" in fifty different languages? Yep, YouTube has that covered too. Maybe you want to learn how to contour your face, cut your own bangs, code your own website, play guitar, or learn how to do a back handspring. You can literally learn how to do all of these things by a quick Google search. The other morning, I was watching *Good Morning America* and saw a story featuring an eight-year-old boy who learned how to drive his father's car by watching a YouTube video so he could take his little sister to McDonald's. Now that is some serious determination, all for a freaking Happy Meal. It's honestly kind of frightening how much you can learn from YouTube—but the point is, the world is literally at your fingertips.

For years, I limited the quality of my blog and video content because I thought things like Photoshop and Final Cut Pro were just too complicated and impossible to understand or learn. So I would end up settling for average-quality content or I would spend way too much money (that I didn't have) paying someone else to design a logo or take photos for me. I had no faith in myself and just chalked it up as "not having the eye" or the skill for it—but really, I just didn't have the patience for it.

That's what it comes down to, girl: patience. It's why so many of us give up on our dreams before we even truly get started. We listen to all of the podcasts, read all of the books, go to all of the personal growth conferences, and then we expect our dream to be built overnight. But that's not how it works. Just because you show up doesn't mean that it's going to be handed to you. You have to put in the work. The day you plant the seed is not the day you eat the fruit—and that's true for your dreams, too.

I thought that moving to Nashville would solve all of my problems. I thought that if I could just get there and wake up every day in Music City, that success would just come knocking on my door. I thought that I would instantly make tons of friends, get invited to all of the cool parties, and exponentially grow my personal brand. But that wasn't the case. I remember a specific Friday night when this reality hit me. At the time, I had lived in Nashville for about three months. I got home from work, sat on my couch, and scrolled Instagram. My feed was filled with videos and photos of my old coworkers back at home, celebrating the end of the workweek at happy hour. My heart sunk. I kept scrolling. It seemed like everyone had plans but me. There I was, sitting in my tiny studio apartment in downtown Nashville all alone, feeling sorry for myself.

Then it hit me: *nothing* had changed. My life was pretty much the same as it was back home in Michigan, except now I was just lonelier. The only thing that had changed was my geographical location. That's it. Same routine, same mindset, same me—just a few states away.

I remember thinking back to what I was told before I left for Nashville. Holly told me to see this new chapter as a "creative hibernation"—and while I *was* hibernating, it definitely wasn't in a creative way. It was more like a bear in the dead of the winter way. I was hitting the snooze button on my dreams, but the truth was I just didn't know how to make them happen. I knew that I needed to be fired up. I knew that I needed to do something that made me uncomfortable, something that intimidated me. I needed to do something *that* night to show up for myself—the girl who packed up her life to head to Nashville to make her dreams a reality. No more snoozing. I wanted to make her proud. I told myself that it was time to start showing up and put in the work.

While I was scrolling Instagram that night, I came across a post that mentioned that Carrie Underwood was playing at the Grand Ole Opry that night. If you're not a country music fan and don't know what the Grand Ole Opry is, it's basically the mecca of country music. Every country legend has performed on that stage. Being a country music lover, it was always a dream of mine to see it in person. My apartment was only about fifteen minutes from the Opry—but I never ended up making it to a show because I didn't have anyone to go with. Going by myself was never even a thought because that would just be humiliating. What kind of weirdo goes to a concert by themselves? Ha, we'll get to that later.

I really wanted to go to the show. But I was terrified of going alone. I went online to see how much tickets were and they were only about thirty dollars. My mind immediately started to race. *Should I go? Should I just do it? Would that be weird? Who would I sit with? Is it weird if I sing out loud by myself?* And then, I snapped myself out of all of the limiting beliefs crowding my mind. I took a deep breath. I bought the ticket. I was finally going to the Grand Ole Opry. Alone.

I remember feeling so silly getting ready. Who was I even getting ready for? Carrie? Psh, yeah sure, we'll go with that. I finished getting ready and drove myself to the Opry, jamming out to Carrie Underwood the entire way. I was scared, but I was proud of myself. I still didn't know how to make my dreams happen, but a part of me felt like I was stepping in the right direction that night.

I remember the walk from the parking lot to the Opry felt as long as a marathon. Everyone was walking in with their dates, their friends, their families—and there I was, looking like I was on a date, but I was really just on a date with myself. I got in, bought myself a double Jack and Diet, and went to go find a seat. The Opry has church pew seating, so I slid in on one of the ends, sat down, and let out a deep breath. I did it. I showed up.

Ironically, I ended up sitting next to some big shot, music industry executive and we hit it off immediately. By the end of the night, he offered me my dream job as Carrie Underwood's social media manager. Just kidding. That definitely didn't happen. But you know what *did* happen? I showed up. I got back in the driver's seat of my own dreams. I took action. I made an effort. It was a small step that gave me the courage and push that I needed. I still didn't know what I was doing, but at least I was doing something.

That's what you need to do, girl. *Something.* Something beyond just moving to your dream city. Something beyond going to the workout class just once. Something beyond just buying the expensive camera. Those are all great first steps, but the magic doesn't happen after the first step. It happens once you put the work in. Once you put *a lot* of work in.

My *me date* to the Opry that night was a turning point for me. I felt empowered. I felt back on track. I felt unstoppable. So that weekend, I pulled out my camera from the bin underneath my bed, blew off the dust, and started filming videos again. But this time around, I wanted to do it differently. I knew that I needed a plan. I knew that I needed consistency. I knew that I needed help. So I did my research. I watched YouTube videos, listened to podcasts, and even took an online course that would help me step up my video editing game. I learned all about domain names, SEO, mailing lists, monetization, and Google analytics. I quickly learned that running a successful personal brand and website wasn't just about snapping pretty photos and posting them on social media—it required work. Did I have a burning passion for SEO and analytics? Hell, no! But I knew that if I wanted to invest in my passion, those were things that I would just have to suck up and learn. They were part of my passion. It's important to understand and accept that fact that just because you are passionate about something, doesn't mean that you are going to love every single second of it. But let me tell you girl, when you start to learn things you didn't think you could, it's empowering. It becomes addicting, too. I remember after I built and launched my first website all on my own, I immediately had a "what's next?" mentality. I wanted to keep growing, keep learning, and keep challenging myself. There's no better feeling than when someone compliments your work and then asks you "Who did that?" and you can finally respond with the answer, "I did."

Out of all of the things that I pushed myself to learn, there was one thing that I always put off. No matter how many things I learned, I told myself that this thing was impossible. I thought that climbing Mount Everest sounded easier than this thing. That thing was Photoshop.

Sounds kind of silly, right? It's not rocket science; it's just Photoshop! But if you've ever attempted to get the hang of Photoshop, I know you feel my pain. It's not intuitive, it seems overly complicated, and it's not exactly cheap. I never even thought about purchasing the program because I knew that I would essentially be paying to end up throwing my laptop into oncoming traffic because of how frustrated I would get trying to learn how to use it.

I saw Nick use Photoshop for everything. No wonder his content was next level—every photo he posted looked like it could be in *National Geographic*. I always just thought it was because he was a natural. When I moved down to Austin and started working for his company, he told me that I should really consider learning how to use Photoshop. I then went on and explained my whole I'd-rather-climb-Mount-Everest spiel in an effort to get out of it. He didn't buy it. He downloaded it onto my computer and sat me down for Photoshop 101.

It sucked. While there were parts that I picked up pretty easily, most parts completely went against my common sense. Cropping a photo seems pretty simple, right? You just select the crop tool and, well, crop the photo. It's as easy as that. Well, not in Photoshop! You have to make sure you have the right layer selected and then go into about forty-two different toolbars to find the crop tool that isn't even called the crop tool and about eighty-six minutes later you finally have a cropped photo. *Yes*, I may be exaggerating—but you get the idea. Photoshop and I weren't exactly besties.

After my first 101 session with Nick, I think I actually felt dumber. It is not a fun feeling. It's a feeling that makes you want to throw your hands up in the air and just hire someone else to do the job for you. But then I would have these little moments where I would remind myself how much more I could accomplish and how much more valuable I could be in my industry if I didn't give up and actually committed to learning how to use Photoshop. So I chose to keep going.

Little by little, I would hit tiny Photoshop milestones. Once I got pretty good at creating graphics for Instagram stories, I gained an inch of confidence. Then, I moved onto logo design. Once I mastered that, I gained another inch of confidence. Then, I moved onto editing photos. One day, we were taking photos for a blog post and as soon as I uploaded the photos, I noticed that I had a coffee stain on the white pants I was wearing. Of course, Nick didn't notice during the shoot because #ManProblems, so I took to Photoshop. I removed that coffee stain like it was my job. You would have never known it was there. I felt proud of myself.

One month. One month was all it took for me to get the hang of it. Did I almost drive to Home Depot just to buy a sledgehammer to smash my laptop because I couldn't figure out how to delete the background from a photo? Absolutely! Did I hate Nick for forcing me to learn how to use Photoshop? Absolutely! But was every single low and frustrating moment worth it? *Absolutely.*

Listen, there will always be people that can do it better, faster, and prettier than you. But guess what? Those people started off just as clueless as you feel in this very moment. I went from not knowing how to import a photo into Photoshop, to designing and creating my entire cookbook from scratch in the program that I once considered "impossible" to learn. It takes time. It takes patience. It takes pushing through the crap days when you want to go buy a sledgehammer at Home Depot to smash your laptop with. I still have days when I can't figure something out in Photoshop and I run to Nick for help. Do you know what his response is on most days? "Well, have you tried Googling it?" And while that response used to make me want to punch him in the face, now it's a reminder to me that everything I've ever wanted to know or learn how to do is just a few clicks away. Sometimes, it's not even a few clicks away, it's just a few words away. Nowadays, there are these know-it-all girls named Alexa and Siri that can give you the answer to literally anything. Well, almost anything. Sometimes, they even get confused.

Maybe it's not Photoshop. Maybe you want to learn how to play the piano or learn how to invest in stocks. Heck, maybe you just want to learn how to do a back handspring because that was your ten-year-old self's dream and it's still locked in your heart.

Believe it or not, Olympic gymnast Shawn Johnson didn't back handspring out of her mother's womb onto the delivery room floor—she had to learn. She had to go beyond just signing up for her first gymnastics class; she had to show up. Again and again. She chose to show up when she didn't want to. She chose to show up when others didn't. She chose to show up because she didn't know how, *yet*. That's the key word here—*yet*. Let that word bring you hope.

It doesn't matter how young or old you are. There's a lot of *yet* in front of you. You haven't started the business, yet. You haven't run the marathon, yet. You haven't found the man of your dreams, yet. You're not a mama, yet. You haven't traveled the world, yet. See how that little word can give your dream so much hope? Start using that little word more. It's going to change your mindset. It's going to push you on the days when you want to give up. All of the things you want to accomplish and all of the things you need to learn in order to accomplish those things, are on the other side of yet.

You may be expecting a structured, bullet-point plan on how to start learning how to do the things you want to do. But the plan is much simpler than that. Don't worry, I'm not going to tell you to Google it—even though that may sometimes be part of it. Just like the last chapter, I want you to pick one thing. One thing that you've always thought you could never do. Once you've picked your thing, start small. Start finding people who have done what you want to do. Learn from them. Go back to their Instagram post from 2014 when it all began. Go ahead, girl, creep away. I won't judge you. There's no shame in following their process if they are where *you* want to be someday. I want you to get obsessed with learning that thing. That one thing. Work towards it little by little, every single day. Accept that there are going to be days where you'll be uncomfortable and that there are going to be days when you are just straight up pissed at the world. But then, out of nowhere, there will be a day, when you do the thing—the *damn* thing, and you are going to be on top of your mountain, already looking for the next one to climb.

CHAPTER 8

The Insecurity: "I Don't Have Help"

Nineteen days ago, I watched one of my biggest dreams come to life right before my very own eyes. I hosted my very first live event, where I stood on a stage and inspired women to live their very best lives. Women flew in from twenty-two different states to hang out with me on a Saturday night in Austin, Texas, and let *me* pep talk them into going after their wild, mountain-moving dreams.

Let's go back to the beginning. One-hundred thirty-four days ago, this event didn't exist. It was just another one of my crazy dreams that I never thought I could pull off on my own. I saw authors, influencers, athletes, and motivational speakers host live events all the time, but they basically had an entire army behind them making it all happen. They have big brands like Whole Foods and

Target begging to sponsor their events. They have event planners, sales managers, logistics coordinators, DJs, stylists, makeup artists, sound engineers, lighting technicians, financial planners, fancy assistants, and probably a whole other list of people with job titles I didn't even know existed. I figured that if I didn't have a team like that behind me, that it was impossible to pull off. So, I never even tried. I was waiting for the right day, the right time, and the right people to come into my life to help make my dream a reality. I kept waiting and waiting—and then one day, it hit me, all thanks to my dad.

My dad is the king of connections. He can't go anywhere without knowing at least three people. I'm serious. Back in the day, my family had to start taking two cars to my brother's hockey games and our school functions because he would need at least an extra thirty minutes just to catch up with everyone he knew. Need a tree cut down in your front yard? Don't worry, my dad knows a guy. Need tickets to the Detroit Red Wings game next weekend? Dad's got you covered. I'm pretty confident that if you wanted to be on NASA's next trip to the moon, my dad would know someone who could get you in. That's how many connections he has.

I was always envious at the number of people my dad had on his team—and by team, I mean his life team. People that he knew and developed relationships with over the years that would drop everything to help him out, or reach out to him when they needed help. So, one day, I asked my dad how he ended up with so many connections and people on his team. He told me that it's just the result of years and years of hard work and showing up. That's when it hit me. A network isn't a prerequisite to doing something. It's a result of something you do.

There I was, doing nothing. No wonder I didn't have all of the connections I wanted or needed. I knew that I needed to do something and the time was now. Team, or no team behind me.

So, I started to make moves without any fancy assistants or event planners. My team leading up to the event consisted of myself, Nick, my mom, and my labradoodle, Ryder. Well, Ryder didn't really do much, but he did offer lots of kisses and moral support along the way. Thanks, Ry.

Remember earlier when I talked about shooting first, and aiming later? That's exactly what I did when it came to this event. I thought that if I committed to it, I could figure it all out along the way. I remember posting a poll on my Instagram story asking the women in my community if they would be interested in an event like this and asked how many would actually attend. I was terrified. I didn't want my secret dream to be shut down—but I knew that I had to gauge my audience to see if this was even a possibility. I told myself that if just fifty girls said yes—I would do it. I figured if I had fifty yeses, hopefully at least twenty-five would actually show up. To be honest, I was just hoping that at least one would show up.

Somehow, I ended up with 478 yeses. I couldn't believe it. Was this really happening? Here I was just hoping for fifty, and I ended up with almost 500. I knew that not all 478 yeses would actually attend, but I was just excited about the possibility to fill the fifty seats I originally dreamed of filling. I couldn't believe *that* many women wanted to come hang out and be inspired by me. There was a moment where I felt like Oprah that was quickly followed by a moment of me kind of wanting to throw up just thinking about it. But the final verdict was in, and I was going for it.

Except, I didn't really know how to go for it. The moment I announced that the event was officially happening was also the moment I really wished I had one of those fancy assistants or event planners. Sure, I had planned school functions and sorority events in the past, but I always had a team or some sort of help backing me up. I had never planned an event like this from scratch, but I knew that I had to start somewhere. I wanted to prove to myself that I could do this, without a fancy team. I wanted this to be my beginning. One day, I wanted to be able to look back at this very moment and remember how far I had come. I didn't know what I was doing, I didn't know how I would be able to do it on my own, but I was determined to find a way.

Pulling something off that you've never done before, without any help requires a lot of backwards planning, which can be terrifying. Backwards planning is essentially committing to something without any idea of how you are actually going to accomplish it. It feels risky. It feels completely right one second and then completely wrong the very second after. But you just have to go with it. So for me, that meant announcing that the event was happening before it even had a date, venue, or even a name. It sounds scary, and even kind of irresponsible, right? Trust me girl, if you feel those things, you are doing it right.

Once I announced that the event was happening, it was time to lock in a date and venue. I decided to give myself four months to plan and pull this thing off. I wanted it to be sometime in the spring, so people could visit Austin before the temperature and humidity levels reached total sauna status. I picked a couple of potential Saturday dates in May and started reaching out to venues to see if they had availability. I had a vision for the venue—I wanted it to be downtown, sophisticated yet chic, and a place where all of the women could feel inspired and comfortable. Well, I quickly found out that my vision was way too expensive for my doing-this-all-on-my-own budget. The first potential venue visit I went on resembled a scene from a scary movie. It was dark, cold, dirty, and smelled like a litter box. I started to panic. How was I supposed to inspire these women in a litter box? Yup, I had officially entered full-on panic mode.

Why was renting a room with four walls and a bathroom so expensive? This was the first official step in planning this event and I already felt like I was failing. All I wanted was someone to tell me what to do. I wanted to give up. But then I remembered, this is my beginning. I had to start somewhere. This was all part of my story. So, I walked out of that first venue visit with my head held high and was determined to find a venue that was in my budget—and preferably one that didn't smell like a litter box.

I got home, put on my event planner hat and got busy Googling. I added words like "low-budget" and "affordable" to my search and found that my options in downtown Austin were pretty slim. But then, I came across a venue that caught my eye. It was a venue and workspace built just for women. My heart started to beat a little faster—this felt like it was meant to be. I clicked on the venue website and immediately fell in love. It was in the heart of downtown Austin. It was all white. It had a beautiful bar and tons of natural light. I thought there was no way this would be in my budget. I sent an email to the venue coordinator just for the fun of it. Maybe it would be a miracle and it would be in my budget. A few hours later, I got an email back. She told me the venue was available on the date I was hoping for and its capacity was more than enough to hold everyone. She attached the pricing sheet to the email. I took a deep breath and opened up the document. Holy freaking guacamole, I could afford this! I immediately emailed her back to set up a meeting so I could see the venue in person. If the pictures were accurate, this could be the one! Well, as long as it didn't smell like a litter box.

I went on the venue visit, and about twenty minutes later, I had a date and venue locked in! It was just what I was looking for. It was a space that was literally made to empower women. It truly felt meant to be. The venue was pretty much an empty space, so I had a lot of work to do. I got home that evening and started to crank out all of the concrete details so I could put tickets up for sale as soon as possible. I had the venue and date locked in; now, I just needed a name for the event. That night in bed as Nick fell asleep in twenty-four seconds per usual while I was doing my usual stare-at-the-ceiling ritual, it came to me. I pulled out my middle-of-the-night inspiration notepad (somehow this is always the time where I get my best ideas) out of my nightstand and wrote down "Best Life Live." It felt right. It embodied everything I wanted the event to be. It was starting to get real.

Now that my event had an identity, it was time to get these tickets on sale so I could plan accordingly once I found out how many women would be attending. It took me days to figure out how much to charge for the tickets. I felt bad charging anything at all, especially since this was my beginning. I didn't know my worth. I was terrified that people would think I was charging too much and tell me to get my head out of the clouds. But at the same time, I didn't want this event to put me in a ton of debt and I needed to cover all of the costs somehow. I asked friends and family what they thought was a reasonable price per ticket and the answers were all across the board and didn't help my decision one bit. Again, I just wanted someone to tell me what to do. I wanted someone to set the ticket price for me. But then I remembered, this is my beginning. I set a ticket price of $50 per ticket and told myself that I was not allowed to change it. The price was set and tickets were about to go on sale.

I researched like crazy to find a ticket-selling platform that didn't take a cut out of each ticket. I was already on a low budget and I needed every cent possible so I could pull this thing off without maxing out my credit card. When the day finally came for tickets to go on sale, I had so many emotions. I had to sell eighty-eight tickets to officially break even from the cost of the venue. I was building a lot of buzz through social media posts, ads, and videos to hit that eighty-eight. I *had* to hit that eighty-eight. I prayed to hit that eighty-eight. And it turns out, I did!

By the time ticket sales closed, I had sold 110 tickets. I couldn't believe it. There I was again, feeling like Oprah. The high was crazy. Selling out my first event was something that I never thought was possible—especially when I was doing it all on my own. But sometimes, life is good and you get the opportunity to blow your own damn mind.

By now, you know what feeling quickly follows the Oprah feeling. Panic. I was only planning on hosting a max of fifty women and now it had more than *doubled*. That meant double the swag bags, double whatever went in the swag bags, double the food, double the wine, which meant double the budget. Well, at least I had one of those fancy financial planners that would keep me on track. Oh wait, yeah that's right, I didn't have one of those. All I had was me, who wasn't exactly the saving type of gal. I blame Amazon Prime.

I had to come up with a plan, and I had to come up with it fast. I had planned on reaching out to a handful of my favorite brands that I already had somewhat of a relationship with to see if they'd want to sponsor a portion of the event, provide a product or service for a giveaway, or include samples or discount codes in the swag bags. How was I supposed to sell them on an event that wasn't even fully put together yet? How was I supposed to ask for 110 samples for free? I was *not* a salesperson. In college, I actually considered sales as a potential career path and even interviewed for a sales-related job and failed miserably. Cold calling? No thanks, I'd rather sit next to a crying baby on a twelve-hour flight. I hated bugging and pushing people. I hated rejection. Therefore, I hated everything I *thought* I knew about sales. But I had to get these brands on board.

I made a list of the dream brands that I would want to be an event sponsor, but I had no plan on how I was going to reach out and actually get a response from these brands. In fact, I didn't even know how to get in touch with them. So, I opened up good ol' Google and got to stalking. Turns out, it's not that hard to get a brand's public relations contact.

I had the list of emails and now it was time to craft the perfect pitch. I was about three lines into my first pitch email before I slammed my laptop shut. It wasn't my style. I sounded like a robot. They probably got hundreds of emails like this per day. Why was I special? Oh yeah, I wasn't. Not if I sent the same, boring pitch email that flooded their inboxes every single day. I had to think outside the box. So, I put my saleswoman hat on and tried to brainstorm a pitch idea that they couldn't ignore.

I tried thinking of my strengths and how I could use

them to grab their attention. I was outgoing, energetic, and enthusiastic—but how was I supposed to get that energy across in an email? Then, it came to me. I set my iPhone on top of a stack of cookbooks on my kitchen table, pressed record and started talking.

I just winged it. I talked about who I was, what I was trying to accomplish with Best Life Live, who my demographic was, why I loved their brand so much, and how being an event sponsor could benefit them. I finished the first video in one take, which was to VICI Collection (one of my favorite clothing boutiques) and watched it back.

It wasn't anything fancy. I was wearing workout clothes and a ball cap. I'm pretty sure I hadn't even taken a shower that day. It was me, the *real* me. I just simply spoke from my heart for three minutes straight, hoping that this approach would catch their eye and work. I felt incredibly vulnerable thinking about someone at VICI opening up their inbox and seeing my face—but if I didn't give it a shot, how was I supposed to ever know if it would have worked? I dropped the video in an email with the subject line of: VIDEO PITCH: Austin, TX Women's Event Sponsor Opportunity, and pressed send.

I heard back from VICI a short four hours later. Four hours! I couldn't believe it. I was terrified to open the email and figured it was probably just an auto-response

"Thanks for your message" email. But it wasn't. This is what the email read:

> Hi Stefany!
>
> Thank you so much for reaching out to us! You are so sweet! We love the video—so creative! We love the idea of the event you are hosting.
>
> We would be happy to offer you an outfit to wear to the event, provide postcards with our info and offer a gift card that you can use for a giveaway/raffle!
>
> Let me know your thoughts!
>
> Best,
>
> Paulina

Holy moly, it worked! It *actually* worked. It felt too easy—I couldn't believe it. Not only did they respond, but they offered way more than I could have ever imagined. The amount of relief I felt in that moment was overwhelming. Maybe I could do this. Maybe I am good at sales. I was on a girl boss high and I didn't want it to go away. So, I picked up the camera, put it back on my makeshift cookbook stack tripod and recorded twenty more videos. Yes, you read that right—*twenty.*

Sure, I could have just made one, generic video and blasted it out to all of the brands at once, but again—that's not who I am. I loved every brand that I was reaching out to for a different reason, and I wanted that to come across in my pitch. I finished recording the videos and sent them off to the rest of the dream brands on my list. After that, all that was left to do was wait.

Within that same week, I received emails back from Soul Cycle and At Home. Before opening the replies, I took a deep breath and reminded myself to set my expectations low. Holy moly. Both brands were on board and so overwhelmingly generous. I let out the giddiest scream. It was working. I never would have thought that such big, fancy brands would want to go out of their way to help me, a twenty-seven-year-old dreamer who they owed nothing to, to help me put on an event to empower women. Did you catch that word in the last sentence? I said help. I was getting *help*. Remember what I said earlier about having a team or connections and how it's not something you are given, it's a result of something you do? Now, I understood it. I was *doing* something, and just like my dad said, the results followed. These brands wanted to be on my team and I was ready to make them proud.

I don't want to leave out mentioning the number of brands that *didn't* want to be on my team. There were tons of brands that either responded with a version of "thanks, but no thanks" or ones that didn't even respond at all. It totally sucks sitting around waiting for an email that you are never going to get—but you have to keep moving forward to find a new plan or solution. Surprisingly, getting rejected didn't suck as bad as I thought it would. When I would get a no—I would just move on and stay motivated by the thought of them one day thinking, "Man, we missed out." I focused on that and moved on. My one-woman show didn't have time to be sad, slowed down, or discouraged.

The confidence that the success from the pitch videos gave me carried me through the entire planning process. That's all it takes. One brave, scary, vulnerable moment that shows you what you are really capable of. Sure, I may have felt awkward, lame, and inexperienced filming and sending off those pitch videos, but without them—I would have never gotten over 110 swag bags donated for free, along with all of the goodies that were inside them. That one, brave, scary, vulnerable moment will unlock your "I can" mentality. We all have it inside of us, but it's up to *you* to unlock it.

Just because I had this newfound confidence didn't mean that everything went smoothly. On my second and final venue visit, I realized that with how the space was laid out, I needed to be elevated in order for the women to see me. I asked the venue if they had a stage and they said no. No worries, I thought, as I looked up local vendors that rented out portable stages. I called a local vendor for pricing and was told that it would be $2,000 to rent the stage, including delivery. $2,000? *Oh hell no*, Steve! I asked the man (Steve) on the phone, if Beyoncé came with the stage for that price and it turns out that Steve wasn't exactly entertained by my humor. Okay fine, I know a Beyoncé-included deal would be way more expensive, but regardless, that price definitely didn't fit in my one-woman-show budget. I needed to put my financial planner hat on, along with my problem-solving hat because I was just two weeks out from my event.

Thanks to my stage crew, AKA my handy fiancé, we came up with a solution. We had a Friday night date night at Home Depot where we spent $200 on lumber, paint, and hardware—came home, cracked open some Coronas, got to work and built the stage from scratch. Take that, Steve.

That Friday night we spent building the stage was a night that I will always remember. In that moment, I wanted to soak it all in. The splinters in my fingers, the paint all over my clothes, my unwashed, sweaty hair underneath my ball cap and the mess we made in our garage that night. This is my beginning. While we were building the stage, I couldn't help but think how metaphoric it was to the dream that I was chasing. Life may not always give you a stage. Sometimes, you just have to build your own. Life may not always give you the right connections or opportunities to bring your dreams to fruition. Sometimes, you just have to be a one-woman-show and create your *own* opportunities.

While I was painting the stage, I had a daydream of me one day in the future, speaking on a stage, a *real* stage, in front of a sold-out, packed audience telling the story about my beginning—and how I had to *literally* build my first stage. That future moment inspired me. It drove me forward.

The final week leading up to Best Life Live was exhausting, but thanks to my Google calendar and to-do list skills, I made it a priority to stay organized in an effort to divert any curveballs that were thrown my way. On the Monday before the event, I set up my version of an assembly line in our living room and stuffed all 110 swag bags by myself. As I was hand stuffing each bag, I feared that the swag bags weren't going to be enough and that the girls were going to be disappointed. The fear paralyzed me for a moment, but I snapped out of it, told myself I was doing my best, and kept going.

On Tuesday, it was time to pick up the entire sound and presentation system that I would use for the event. Yeah, the venue didn't provide any of that, either. This was a day that I was kind of dreading. I barely knew an HDMI cord from a USB cord; how was I supposed to success-fully set up a sound system? I walked into the shop and immediately felt out of place and insecure. I was dressed head-to-toe in Lululemon with my printed checklist in hand of everything I needed. Everyone ahead of me in line looked like they were the lead singer of a rock band and sounded like they knew exactly what they were talking about. Then here I was, looking like workout Barbie just hoping that I wouldn't screw this up. When it was my turn to be helped, I wasn't really sure if I should use the "fake it until you make it" approach so I wouldn't look like a total idiot, or just be completely transparent and tell these guys I had absolutely no idea what I was doing. It only took thirty seconds for the sound guy to drop a word I had never heard of, which resulted in me confessing that I was totally clueless. He smiled, told me not to worry, and assured me that he was there to help.

There's that word again. Help. He was *helping* me. The sound guy at that shop may have not known it in that moment, but he was officially on my team. He was going to help me pull this off. I pulled out my phone and filmed him going through every piece of equipment, so I would know what plug goes where, what level to turn each knob to and so on. At the end of the appointment, he told me that he really appreciated me being honest about not being familiar with the equipment. He said it ends up being more work for them in the long run if people pretend they know what they are doing, because they either break the equipment or call the day of the event, panicking for last-minute instructions. In that moment, I realized how overrated it was to fake it until you make it. Here's the thing about that common concept we are always told to do when faced with tackling something we aren't an expert in: it's *exhausting*. It's anxiety-inducing. No one will teach you if they think you already know everything—and that's why it's so important to embrace the I-don't-knows. The sooner you are honest about the things you don't know how to do, the sooner you will learn how to actually do them.

The rest of the week leading up to the big day on Saturday went surprisingly smooth. Thursday night, Nick and I made a trip to Costco to purchase all of the wine for the event. I tried as hard as I possibly could to get a wine sponsor for the event, but it turns out that wasn't so easy. So, we left Costco with forty-plus bottles of wine, hand-selected and paid for by none other than yours truly. At that point, my budget wasn't exactly happy with me. Let's just put it that way.

When Friday came along, it was go-time. The rest of my team flew in—and by team I mean my mom, who was going to be my right-hand man for everything; my sister, who was going to help with setup and check-in; my sister's boyfriend, Steve, who was in charge of all sound and music; my friend Holly, who was hosting a portion of the event; and our friend Joe, who was going to be the in-house bartender for the evening.

My team was small but mighty. They understood my dream. They chose to *help* me make my dream a real, living, breathing thing. Even through all of my day-of anxiety and last-minute panic attacks, from setup to takedown, they were on my team. Just an hour before the doors opened, I gathered my team for one final toast and one final thank you for all they had done for me. As I was giving my toast, I looked around at the six people who had shown up for me. In that moment, I had everything I needed. It turns out that I didn't need a fancy assistant, event planner, sales manager, or financial planner. Everything I needed for my beginning was right in front of me. We raised our glasses to new beginnings and dreams coming true, and opened the doors.

Best Life Live was everything I had ever dreamed of and more. We danced, we hugged, we laughed, we cried, we lifted each other up—and I am confident that every single woman walked out of those doors at the end of the night a better version of themselves, including me. If you would have told me just *one* year ago that I would stand on a stage, that I built, inspiring one-hundred-plus women to live their best lives, I would have never believed you. I would have told you that it was impossible to do on my own. I would have told you that it was too scary, too expensive, and way too much work. Well guess what girl, it was *all* of those things. I was terrified every step of the way. I went way over my budget and completely underestimated the amount of work it required to successfully pull it off. But I *did* it. From the signs, to the swag bags, to the napkins, to the stage setup (which was literally my living room furniture)—I designed and did it all. Every little imperfect part of it.

When the moment comes where you can actually look and physically see your dream come to life, every little bump along the way completely smooths out and disappears. It all becomes worth it. I learned more from this experience than any podcast, book, or motivational speech could ever teach me. You learn by *doing* things, and sometimes you have to do those things without a team of experts or professionals. You make do with what you have.

Girl, I hear you when you say that you don't have the help. I get it. But I'm going to make a correction to that sentence. You don't have the help *yet*. Remember all of the hope that little word can bring you? You don't have help *yet*. And that's okay. Help comes when you do something to inspire it. There are people in your life who want to see you succeed. They want to share your vision and help you bring it to life. But you won't find those people until they see you take those first, brave steps on your own. Remember, sometimes the smallest step in the right direction ends up being the biggest step of your life.

CHAPTER 9

The Insecurity: "I Don't Deserve It"

Have you ever been to Target at 2 p.m. on a Monday? Well, it's a different experience than your post-workday or weekend Target run, where the aisles are filled to the brim with moms and their kids still dressed in their muddy soccer uniforms. A Monday at 2 p.m. is a totally different vibe. It's filled with retired women living their best lives and stay-at-home moms with their Starbucks in hand, wandering the aisles while enjoying the peace and quiet away from their children. To be honest, it's quite serene. Up until a year and a half ago, I didn't know that this sacred time at Target even existed because I was working my nine-to-five job, Monday through Friday.

I'll never forget my first Monday after quitting my nine-to-five job in Nashville. It was the first time in four years that I didn't wake up to an alarm and it felt weird. When I did wake up, panic rushed through my body because I thought I had overslept and was going to be late for work. Once I took myself off autopilot and remembered that I didn't have a nine-to-five job to get to, I got out of bed and looked out my bedroom window, which overlooked 11th Avenue in the heart of The Gulch. I saw men in suits walking out of Killebrew Coffee with their morning cup of joe to-go, along with a ton of other people on their phones, with their backpacks on and briefcases in hand looking like they were headed to work. Then, I took a glance at myself in the mirror. I was braless, wearing my oversized toothpaste-stained Smashville T-shirt with floral boxer shorts, sporting hair that looked like it had been through a car wash, all while rocking my retainers. It was quite the look if I do say so myself.

Just as I finished making coffee, I reached into the cabinet to grab my to-go thermos. I quickly stopped myself, as I remembered that I wasn't going anywhere. I snapped back out of autopilot mode and put the thermos back in the cabinet. I poured my coffee into a mug and made my way to the couch and turned on *Good Morning America*. As I was slowly sipping my cup of coffee listening to Robin Roberts and Michael Strahan, this overwhelming sense of anxiety came over me. Sitting on the couch drinking my cup of coffee on a Monday morning just felt wrong. I felt guilty. All of my friends and family were busy at their jobs while I was sitting here watching a morning news segment about Keto recipes. The guilt got to me, so I got up off the couch, made some breakfast, and started to pack up my things in preparation for my big move to Austin next week. A few hours into packing, I decided to head to Target to pick up some storage containers (and probably a list of other nonsense things I didn't need because, well—#TargetProblems) to organize my things for the move.

That was the first time I experienced the 2 p.m. on a Monday sacred time at Target. While I too thoroughly enjoyed strolling the aisles with my tall vanilla latte, I still felt anxious. I still felt guilty. The store felt like a ghost town, with the exception of a few moms who were loading their carts up with obscene amounts of paper towels and toilet paper. The cherry on top of my insecurity sundae was when the cashier asked me if I was a student at Belmont or Vanderbilt. Nope. Just trying to get some containers to organize my life in so I can move to Austin and go after my dream, lady. Move along now.

In a world where the nine-to-five corporate life is the norm, it's assumed that all twenty-something aged people are at work at 2 p.m. on a Monday. I walked out of Target feely guilty, knowing that my new flexible schedule and lifestyle change would take some time getting used to. In that moment, I didn't feel like I deserved a flexible schedule that allowed me to be at Target in the middle of a workday. I wish I could tell you that that was the one and only time that I experienced that guilty, I-don't-deserve-this feeling, but the truth is, it's something I still feel and battle with today.

What I was feeling that day was something called imposter syndrome. Have you ever felt like you don't deserve your accomplishments? Or that you are worried that people will think you're a fraud, even though you know you're not? That's the annoying beast that imposter syndrome is. It's the idea that you believe that you've only succeeded because of luck, and not because of your talent or hard work. You could accomplish one of your biggest goals—but at the end of the day you still feel a sense of guilt for being successful. It sounds kind of crazy, doesn't it? As women, not only do we face feelings of being insecure and unworthy when we want to go for the big promotion or new career change, we face the exact same feelings when we are *actually* successful at it. Now, that's really crazy.

The first few months of my new lifestyle change and career path were the most challenging ones. At that point, Nick had been an entrepreneur and essentially his own boss for about three years, so this was his normal and therefore no big deal. However, waking up whenever you want, working on whatever you want and not reporting to a big scary boss was *not* my normal. I constantly felt like I was doing something wrong. Or that I wasn't doing enough. Don't get me wrong, I loved my newfound creative freedom and working with Nick—we made a great team. I brought new creative perspectives on marketing, social media, and content creation and he was insanely talented when it came to executing it. No matter how hard we worked or how many hours we spent behind our laptops, at the end of each day—I still felt like I was never doing enough. For the first couple of months, I didn't even think about working on my blog content or cookbook. I was afraid that if I spent too much time working on non-Bare Performance Nutrition projects for my own personal brand and goals, Nick would feel like I was just taking advantage of him or using him. I also worried about what everyone else thought, too. By everyone else—I mean my family and friends, Nick's family and friends, and oh yeah, the 400,000+ people that followed Nick on social media.

I would constantly run through scenarios in my head of what people would think. I convinced myself that they were thinking, "Who is this girl? She's just dating Nick to use him to get more followers!" or, "She's just using him for his money! She's a gold digger!" While all of those statements were fabricated by my own insecurities and *completely* false, I convinced myself that those were real things people were thinking and saying about me.

The only thing that's worse than imagining the judgmental things people say about you is when they *actually* say them. I'll never forget a text that I got from someone who I considered to be a good friend. It was a month or so after my move to Austin and she sent me a few texts in a row before I saw them and got the chance to respond. The last text she sent read, "LOL sorry for blowing you up, but I guess it's not like you're working anyway!"

As soon as I read that last text, my heart immediately sunk. It stung. *Bad.* I had never felt so misunderstood as I did in that moment. Certain people just didn't get it. I didn't expect them to get it—but I did hope for support from my friends and family. I knew it was difficult for all of the nine-to-five warriors to wrap their heads around the fact that I created my own schedule and I could wear my pajamas all day if I wanted to, but I didn't expect to get a text like that from a friend. Yes, I may have read too far into it and she probably didn't intend for the text to hurt me, but it was just fuel to my insecurity fire that I was trying my best to put out.

The fuel kept on coming. The sting came back at my cousin's wedding in a conversation Nick and I were having with one of my extended family members. It was her first time meeting Nick and it only took about two minutes for her to raise concerns about our lifestyle. She said she just "didn't get what we do for a living" and hoped we had healthcare. I was embarrassed that one of my family members would ask a question like that. If it was up to me, I would have gone into full-defense-mode in an effort to explain to her all that we do, how hard we work, and how much growth and success we were experiencing. But as soon as I glanced over at Nick and immediately read the "don't waste your breath" look on his face, I knew he was right—I didn't owe an explanation to a third cousin that I only saw at weddings and funerals.

Fast-forward about nine months after I moved to Austin, I had *finally* started feeling confident enough to start working towards my personal goals again. I had finished two cookbooks, my blog was completely revamped and a living, breathing thing again, and I was finally starting to build a community of amazing, like-minded women. The sting was fading and I finally felt like my girl boss, I-deserve-this self again.

But then just like that, the sting came back and it was the biggest sting of all. It came from a review left on our podcast a few months after we launched it. Nick and I covered topics like relationships, business, health, fitness and so on. Up until that point, we hadn't received one negative review. We knew we were bound to get one eventually; I just didn't think it would be so directed towards me. Whoever wrote the review apparently had a lot of time on their hands because it was four whole paragraphs long. Here's the part of the review that left the sting:

> *Stefany would be so much more "marketable" just being the fiancé of Nick. She needs to embrace that role rather than trying to squeeze into his entrepreneurial success as her own. Stef, just be yourself and find something you enjoy and just stick to that. You're all over the place every other week in some new area with no experience to back it up.*

When I read the review for the first time, my heart broke a little. *Okay,* so it shattered into pieces onto my keyboard. Every insecurity, every doubt, every I-don't-deserve-this thought I had ever had felt validated. It felt real and true. I felt like a fraud. I felt defeated, and I let myself believe every word that stranger wrote about me.

I threw myself a pity party for about five minutes where I decided to personally torture myself by reading the review over and over again, overanalyzing every single word. After the pity party was over, I did what any twenty-something girl would do and called my mom. Because she's my mom and we talked on the phone at least twice a day, she knew that every line of that review was a direct jab to each and every one of my insecurities. I could tell that the review hurt my mom almost as much as it hurt me, because she knew how hard I worked and how passionate I was about the work that I was doing. Like any great mom, she calmed me down and tried her best to convince me that all of the things that were said in the review weren't true and that it was probably written by a terrible person. I hung up the phone but still felt that sting. I let that *one* bad review drain all of my motivation, passion, and purpose. I was ready to give up, delete my blog and social media, and start applying for nine-to-five jobs again. I didn't feel worthy of the life I had been living for the last few months.

When I read the review to Nick, he didn't seem the least bit phased and didn't express one ounce of sympathy for me. Frankly, it pissed me off. Couldn't he tell how devastated I was? Didn't he care about me? Why wasn't he comforting me? But as soon as he started talking, my entire perspective was changed and I had reached a tremendous turning point in my life that has now made me grateful for that terrible podcast review. You read that right. Today, I'm grateful for that bad review.

When Nick and I were talking about the review, he went on to congratulate me on my first "hater." Okay, now he was *really* starting to piss me off. Congratulations? Really? I wasn't exactly in the tough love, sarcastic mood. He then went on to tell me that it's a good thing that I had a hater, because it meant that I was actually standing up for something in my life and that I wasn't playing it safe to make everyone *else* happy. And just like that, my entire perspective changed. He was right. For the first time in a long time, I was finally staying true to myself rather than conforming to what everyone else wanted me to do, post, or say.

I've never been a one-size-fits-all type of gal when it comes to the things that I am passionate about in life. I've learned that being a multi-passionate person is by no means easy in a society where everyone wants to fit you in one box, and that one box only. But I didn't fit into one box. I didn't even fit into two or three boxes. Somedays, I woke up and wanted to film cooking videos and write cookbooks. The next day, I would wake up and want to film one of my workouts to help girls who didn't know where to get started in the gym. There were days when I wanted to teach girls how to decorate their home, and days where I wanted to give them pep talks about self-love and confidence. There was even a day that I stood on a stage in front of one-hundred-plus women and inspired them to live their best lives. I didn't fit into one genre, category, or industry. I didn't fit into one box and I know that I never will. And I'm okay with that, because having more than one box was what gave me fulfillment, opportunity, and ultimately success.

At first, the bad review without a doubt brought back the imposter syndrome in me. It made me feel like a fraud and tricked me into believing that none of the success I was experiencing was actually mine. But then, I learned something really valuable from this "hater" of mine.

It taught me that winners focus on winning, and losers focus on winners. In this case, that person who wrote the review was the loser. That day, I decided that I was going to try my absolute hardest to not spend one more millisecond of my life being held hostage by the insecurity of thinking that my wins didn't belong to *me*. I said "try" because I'm still working at it, but I've come a long way.

Did dating Nick help grow my platforms and teach me a lot about how to become successful? Abso-freaking-lutely. But did Nick do the work that got me my first brand deal, or the work that filled one-hundred-plus seats at my first public speaking event? Abso-freaking-lutely not. That was me. All me, girl. And today, I am *finally* starting to realize that. And I'm damn proud of it.

For the first year, all of the stings prevented me from ever completely shaking the I-don't-deserve-it mentality and insecurities that came with it. Even after all of the encouragement I got from Nick to finish my cookbooks and continue to grow my blog and personal brand, it still felt wrong. I was afraid that any success that I *did* create for myself would always be credited to the luck and opportunities that came along once I started dating Nick. I knew that these things weren't true, but my imposter syndrome brainwashed me into thinking that I didn't deserve any of it.

Here's the thing about the people who tell me that I "lucked out"—they don't realize how long I've been chipping away at this dream of mine because they didn't *see* me then. To them, the start of my existence as a human being was when I started dating Nick. They didn't see me staying in from fraternity parties in college to meet a deadline for the university newspaper I wrote for. They didn't see me spend all of my free time outside of my nine-to-five job learning how to film and edit videos. They didn't see the *years* of trial and error. That's the thing about the dream you're trying to chase—you have to do a lot of the work in silence. Your success is what will make the noise, and no matter what—some people just don't want to hear it.

There's an illustration that is called "The Iceberg Illusion" that paints the perfect picture of what success is really like. Think of what an iceberg looks like: it has two parts. It has a part that people can see, above the surface—and a part that people can't see, below the surface. In the illustration, the part that we can see above the surface is the success. The part that we can't see below the surface, is everything it took to achieve that success. Things like sacrifice, failures, setbacks, late nights, early mornings, failure, persistence, and dedication. We often get mesmerized and even jealous by someone's "above the surface" without even factoring in everything they had to endure below the surface to get there. Out of sight, out of mind.

I'm sure you've heard it before, but we live in a time of the highlight reel. Let's be real here. Most people don't include that below-the-surface stuff in their highlight reels, because it sucks. It's part of the struggle. No one wants to admit that they're struggling. On social media, we see the promotions, not the hours put in. We see the trophies, not the sweat. We see the big houses and fancy trips but not the sacrifices that were made. So yeah, nowadays you may see me at Target at 2 p.m. on a Monday, but what you didn't see was me working my ass off on my Saturday and Sunday to hit a deadline or finish a project.

At the beginning of this chapter, I mentioned how feeling unworthy and undeserving of my life is still something that I battle with today, and it's true. I've made tremendous progress and learned how to turn off my imposter syndrome in certain scenarios, but there are still days or conversations I have with people that bring back that I-don't-deserve-this feeling. Whenever Nick and I return to our hometowns, which are both pretty conservative small towns, we both tend to feel like we are outcasts and that we no longer "fit the mold." We're back in a place that's surrounded by the nine-to-five, 401(k)s, PTO, and a lot of people that have been counting down the days until retirement since their first day on the job, because they have no passion for what they do. Nick's really good at letting this feeling fuel him—he uses it as a reminder of how lucky we are to have created our own careers from the ground up. It also gives him an extra boost of motivation, because just a few years ago he was in that world, and he has no plans of ever going back.

And then there's me. The overthinking, recovering-people-pleaser gal that a lot of us tend to be. When I'm back home and feel that outcast, don't-fit-the-mold feeling, I get sucked back into the nine-to-five corporate stigma and realize how different my lifestyle really is, and I end up feeling guilty for it. I see some of my best friends only live for the weekends. I see my own mother stressed beyond belief because of the pressure her career has put on her for twenty-plus years, in a field that she isn't even passionate about. It breaks my heart a little bit and it leaves me wondering, *why me?* Why was *I* the one who got to make her own schedule and wake up every morning with a fire in her heart because she loved what she did? Why was *I* the one who didn't have to stress about PTO days or a controlling boss every time she wanted to take a vacation? Why did *I* get the opportunity to live a life that some of my friends and family dreamed of? Why me?

This "why me" feeling has caused me to downplay not

only my success but my overall happiness every time I'm around or speaking to someone that I know isn't fulfilled with their own life. There I was again, making myself small to make everyone else around me feel comfortable. I wouldn't talk about my goals or dreams, and I felt awkward or guilty talking about my latest brand deal or the next big project I was working on. Anytime I would receive a compliment or acknowledgment about my accomplishments, I would always respond with a "Thank you, but..." and downplay the hard work I put in. I didn't want them to feel small—so instead, I made myself small.

Girl, if you've made it this far into the book, I know that you are *not* small. I'm going to say it again, so you can get your highlighter out and highlight the crap out of the next sentence. You are *not* small. Neither are your dreams. So, don't you dare shrink yourself for someone else's comfort. Don't feel guilty for finally getting the promotion that you deserved months ago. Don't feel guilty for taking a vacation that's not a holiday break. Don't feel guilty for finally quitting the job that you hate, to pursue a passion that you love. Don't feel guilty for being a stay-at-home mom while all of your friends are working their nine-to-five jobs. Don't feel guilty for loving your life. Joy is not an emotion that should ever be suppressed. If anything, we need more of it in this world. You deserve every ounce of joy that comes into your life, because you only have one life. Stop wasting your days overthinking, feeling guilty, and wondering if your success is due to luck, rather than the hard work you put in. At the end of the day, it's the one and only life you've been given, so you must make the most of it. Own your life. Own the opportunities it gives you. Own the joy you feel from it.

Owning your life and the success you've earned isn't always easy. It's crazy how difficult feeling what you *actually* feel can be. I had an imposter syndrome moment right after Best Life Live wrapped up. I had just gotten off stage and finished taking photos and hugging more than one-hundred girls. After taking everything down, cleaning up the venue, and loading it all back into the U-Haul, I got into the car with my mom and sister to head back home around midnight. As soon as the car doors shut, my mom and sister immediately asked how I felt with an insane amount of excitement and anticipation in their voices. I knew that they expected an answer like "incredible" or "proud" to come out of me, but the only word I could use to describe how I felt in that moment, just one hour after one of my dreams had come true, was *anxious*.

As soon as it was all over, I felt this tremendously heavy weight on my heart. I spent the last five hours meeting, hugging, and talking to women who traveled from twenty-two different states just to meet *me*. They told me stories about how I motivated them to do something they thought they could never do, how much joy I bring into their lives, and how thankful they were that I always kept things "real" on social media. Those are all incredible affirmations. All I ever wanted was to inspire and help women improve their lives, and I was finally doing it—so why did I feel so anxious?

I explained to my mom and sister that it was really overwhelming having these women show up from all across the country, just for me. I wasn't Oprah. I didn't have a million followers on Instagram. I didn't start a multimillion-dollar business. I wasn't an expert or a guru. I was just a twenty-seven-year-old girl who still wears her retainers at night, occasionally burns dinner, and still couldn't keep a plant alive to save her life. So why were these incredible women showing up to be inspired by *me?* This was imposter syndrome at its finest.

That night, I told myself that I could never put on another event like that again. It felt like too much emotional responsibility. There I was, standing on a stage inspiring a crowd of women to live their best lives, when there were still days I felt like I hadn't even figured out how to do that for myself yet. When I was on stage, I really *did* feel like Oprah, but as soon as the energy faded and the chaos settled and I had time to reflect in my own head—I felt like a fraud.

Before falling asleep that night, I opened up my email

and social media and got bombarded with messages and social media posts from women who were at Best Life Live, saying how much they enjoyed it and were already asking when the next one would be. I turned my phone off and went to bed hoping I could sleep off the imposter syndrome.

Thankfully, somehow and some way, I did. When I woke up the next morning, the weight on my heart had been lifted and both my mind and purpose were clearer than ever. All I wanted to do that very day was start planning my next event so I could inspire even more women.

When I walked into the kitchen the morning after Best Life Live, everyone was recapping and reliving the night over coffee. Again, I was asked how I felt now that it was all over. I could tell my mom was anxiously anticipating my answer to see if it had changed since last night's car ride home. When I told her how much better I felt, she told me that she knew the feelings of overwhelm and anxiety would disappear and that I just needed some time to come down from the exciting, overwhelming high that Best Life Live was. And she was right. Moms are always right.

While you are working towards those mountain-moving dreams of yours, you are going to experience the highest of the highs, followed by the lowest of the lows. One minute, everything is going to feel right—and the next, it's all going to feel absolutely wrong. You're going to have your Oprah moments, followed by your I'm-a-fraud moments. But that's all part of it, girl. It's all a head game—and you can't let fear get in the way of your purpose.

When good things happen to you along your journey, because they will, don't question if you deserve it or not. Feeling undeserving creates resistance to positive change. Listen girl, it *happened*. It's done. It can't un-happen, so take the hand you've been dealt and make the absolute most of it. If imposter syndrome comes knocking on your door, that's okay—here's what I want you to do when that happens:

IDENTIFY IT

Answer the door, say hi, and acknowledge that imposter syndrome came for a visit. The first step is recognition and identifying what is shaking your confidence. Breaking down exactly why you are feeling this way can be tremendously freeing. Let's say you got a promotion at the company you've only been working at for three months. There's a handful of other employees who have been there longer and they haven't received promotions yet. Identify why you feel like you don't deserve it. Chances are, you may be feeling that way because so-and-so has worked there longer or is more experienced. Sure, you may be a newer employee—but *you* got the promotion, and you got it for a reason.

REMIND YOURSELF OF YOUR WINS

Take a moment and look back at everything you've achieved, and reflect on all of the late nights, early mornings, and hard work you've put in to get to where you are now. Like I mentioned, you got the promotion for a reason—so remind yourself of those reasons. Embrace the fact that you got yourself to where you are. You've earned your spot. Your success is proof of that. If this is a hard step for you to conquer, make yourself a "win" jar. Every single win, big or small—write it down and put it in the jar. On days where imposter syndrome is getting the best of you, pick out one of the wins. Remind yourself that you deserve it, but at the same time—don't let it slow you down. Don't let the wins get to your head so much that you become complacent. Remember that wins are in the *past*. You have to keep working for the new, bigger, better wins. Let the reminder fuel you and leave you hungry for more.

ACCEPT PRAISE

Stop adding "buts" to the end of your responses when you're accepting a compliment. "Thanks, but...I just got lucky." Or "Thanks, but...it's not a big deal." Stop it, right now! You're putting yourself in that tiny little box again. You don't belong there, remember? We underestimate how much the words we say out loud can actually impact the way we feel. Every time you're about to brush off a compliment, stop yourself and just say "Thank you." Not a single word after that, got it?

Little by little, those three tactics are going to help you fight off imposter syndrome. It's *so* important to recognize and respect your talent and worth every single step of the way. Even when it feels like others don't—you need to show up for yourself. Remember that the people who attack your confidence, character, and self-esteem are the ones who are aware of your potential, even if you are not.

Let this chapter be a reminder that you should always be your biggest cheerleader. Negotiate the salary. Be proud of your promotion. Rock the Louis Vuitton handbag you worked hard for, even if it's just to Walgreens. Hell, go to Target at 2 p.m. on a Monday and enjoy every single second of it because girl, you deserve it.

CHAPTER 10

"I'll Do It Later"

When I started writing this book, this chapter didn't exist. It wasn't in the outline. It wasn't even a thought because at that point, it wasn't a lesson that I had learned yet. But one month ago, to the day, everything changed. This chapter went from not existing, to being the most important one out of the entire book. It's not really an insecurity—but it's something we all tell ourselves when it comes to our dream. This chapter is the biggest challenge for me to write, but it's also the chapter with the most important lesson that you will learn.

We've all heard the icebreaker question, "What would you do if you were told you had one week left to live?" It can tell you a lot about someone and what matters most to them. Some would choose to spend it with family, while some would spend it traveling the world. Others would quit their job and start checking things off their bucket list—and maybe a few wouldn't change a thing at all. It's a question that we never take too seriously, because as humans, we tend to think that we are invincible. We think that *we* are in charge of the time we are blessed with on this earth. So we book vacations months in advance. We make five-year plans. We make ten-year plans. We plan our weddings months or sometimes even years in advance. We have all of these things that we want to do, that we want to accomplish, but we figure we have all the time in the world—so, we say we'll do it later. But here's the thing about "later"—I've recently learned that it isn't guaranteed.

One month ago, to the day, on June 10, 2019, Nick's mother and my future mother-in-law, Linda, had her "later" taken from her. She was fifty-seven-years-young and had a whole lot of "later" left to live. She had retirement to celebrate, vacations to enjoy, her son's wedding, and future grandbabies to help raise and love. But for a reason that we will never understand, she was robbed of all of those special moments.

Only six months earlier, Linda got the news that she had been diagnosed with Stage 3 ovarian cancer. It didn't make sense to any of us. She was truly the vision of health—she was a runner, she coached Special Olympics, she ate healthy, she was always trying to be the absolute best version of herself. She was fifty-seven, going on thirty.

It's always a relatively nerve-racking moment when you meet your boyfriend's mother for the first time. What made it even more nerve-racking for me was the fact that Linda was a boy-mom. In fact, the whole extended Bare family was pretty much men. Even before I met her, it was pretty obvious how much she loved and protected her boys, and how much they loved and protected her, right back. Nick and I flew to Pennsylvania for the big "meet the parents" weekend. I had knots in my stomach the entire plane ride. I had never had a boyfriend before Nick, which obviously meant that I had never met a boy-friend's parents before. Would they like me? Would they think that I was a good match for their son? What if I talked too much? Or what if I talked too little? Were the outfits I brought appropriate enough? The list of worries went on and on.

When Nick and I arrived to baggage claim in Pennsyl-vania, I went to the bathroom to freshen up while Nick waited for our bags. When I got back, I saw Nick stand-ing with both of our suitcases and noticed that he was wearing an interesting smirk on his face. It was the kind of smirk that said, "She's going to freak."

As soon as I asked him what was going on, he told me not to panic. In that very moment I got an intense whiff of Cabernet Sauvignon. "Yeah, you known that bottle of wine from Traverse City you brought for my mom? Well, it broke in my suitcase. But it's okay—I can wash everything as soon as we get to my parent's house!"

Great. This trip was already off to a fabulous start. I pictured the moment I met his parents. "Hey, Mr. and Mrs. Bare! Nice to meet you! Sorry I smell like an alcoholic and that the gift I brought for you is destroyed. Oh, and by the way, can we use your washer?" It felt like one of those moments you would only see in a movie or read in a book (ha!)—but I needed to keep my cool because I was about to meet my potential future in-laws in about forty-five seconds.

Nick's parents pulled up outside of the airport and I'm pretty sure Linda jumped out of the car before it had even come to a complete stop. I'll never forget the way she squealed my name and lunged towards me with open arms, before even hugging her own son. She made every nervous feeling in my body disappear in an instant. There was something special about her. I felt it in her hug.

It only took about thirty seconds into the car ride home for her to tell me that she was throwing me a party. Yes, you read that right. A party. This woman, who hadn't even known me for a full two minutes yet, was throwing me a party. She told us the party was going to be on Saturday night, and all of their friends and practically the entire neighborhood was coming because they were so excited to see Nick and meet me for the first time. Dang, it sounded like this gal knew how to throw a party.

When we got back to their house, we munched on pistachios and drank Shocktops while we all talked out by their pool. She asked about my family, friends, my time living in Nashville, and where I learned to cook so well (she obviously had creeped my Instagram). While she was asking all of these questions about me and my life, I couldn't really focus because I just wanted to know more about her. She had this light to her that was just so comforting. She reminded me of my mom. I swear I could feel the warmth on my skin. That's how kind she was. I remember looking at Nick and realizing how much it all made sense now. This is where he got it from.

The weekend was incredible. And let me tell you, I wasn't exaggerating when I said that Linda knew how to throw a party. Unfortunately, it stormed the entire night, but that didn't stop what felt like the entire town from coming to one of Linda's legendary house parties. I'm serious, there had to be at least one-hundred people who came in and out of their basement that night. We drank, we ate, we played games— she made it feel like I had been a part of their family forever. Prior to that weekend, I was almost positive that Nick was "the one," but after that weekend, I couldn't have been more sure. I knew leaving that weekend that I hadn't just met my boyfriend's parents—I had met my future in-laws.

I know that the term "mother-in-law" sometimes comes with a negative stigma. I mean, have you ever seen the movie, *Monster-In-Law*? Yeah, it doesn't exactly make you thrilled about the day you finally meet your future mother-in-law. Everyone has heard the horror stories about the turbulent relationships between a mother-in-law and her daughter-in-law. The stories are always along the lines of the mother-in-law not approving or never thinking any woman would be "good enough" for her son, or how she tries to control the relationship and how her grandchildren are raised. It's a real issue that even a lot of my own girlfriends have to deal with but not me. I knew within minutes of meeting Linda that I was one of the lucky ones. I knew that one day she wouldn't just be my mother-in-law—she would be my friend. And for the short amount of time I was blessed to have with Linda, that's exactly what she was. My friend.

You know that friend who just makes everything a party? You could be doing something torturous, like getting a tooth pulled—but as long as you had that friend by your side, you would be all "bring on the Novocain!" and make a party out of it. That's the kind of person Linda was. Last fall, we were at a wedding and I was standing in line at the bar with her to get a drink. When the bartender asked what she wanted, she said, "Oh gosh, I don't know, just something fruity with vodka!" I told the bartender to make that two as we waited on our custom cocktails.

When we took the first sip, we gave the bartender a round of applause because it was freaking delicious. Soon enough, everyone in line behind us was intrigued and started to order the same thing. When we came back for round two, the bartender told Linda that she had started a movement—everyone was ordering her drink! He asked for her name, and officially named the drink "The Linda," and by the end of the night, I'm pretty sure 80 percent of the wedding guests were drunk off of Lindas. It was amazing. She truly brought the fun everywhere she went.

And that was the exact reason how we knew something wasn't right with her health—in the fall of 2018, we could tell that she was fighting to keep up with her usual fun, high-energy self. Nick's parents came down to Texas to help with our big Black Friday sale, like they have in the past for a lot of our big sales. Usually, Linda is doing laps around us all restocking shelves, helping pack orders, and making sure everyone stays fed and energized during the long days. But that Thanksgiving, things were different. She had mentioned that she hadn't "felt right" for a while—but figured it was some kind of stomach bug or it had something to do with the stress of starting her new position at work. She shook it off and still tried to keep up with everyone during the Black Friday sale madness. She couldn't make it more than an hour before she had to lie on the couch in the front office to take a nap. Something was off and it was really starting to make us nervous.

We really knew something was up when she didn't have enough energy to cook up the big Thanksgiving dinner she had planned on making everyone. It wasn't like Linda. She loved to cook. She loved to take care of people. But that Thanksgiving, we had a feeling that we might have to start taking care of her.

The months following Thanksgiving were an emotional roller coaster. The doctors had found a blood clot in her lung and from there, Linda was constantly in and out of doctor appointments in an attempt to finally figure out why she wasn't feeling like her usual self. In December, we were all supposed to head to their family's cabin for the weekend, but as soon as Nick and I landed at the airport, Nick's dad called us and said that they received some news and that Linda wouldn't be able to join us at the cabin that weekend. When we finally saw Linda, she was still fighting to remain as positive as possible. She told us that "some number" in her test results was higher than it was supposed to be and that the doctor didn't want her going anywhere that wasn't near a hospital in case of an emergency. While that scared all of us, she remained calm and said it wasn't a big deal, and insisted that we still go to the cabin. Of course, we refused to go without her, but of course she *made* us go—with a car full of food that she had prepared for the weekend. Typical Linda.

In late January after things weren't getting better, Linda

had an exploratory surgery to give us the results we were all waiting months for. I'll never forget the call that we got from Nick's dad, telling us that the surgeon had found aggressive cancer cells in her abdomen. She was diagnosed with stage 3 ovarian cancer and started her first round of chemo immediately. It certainly wasn't easy getting the news from halfway across the country—and of course, both Nick and his brother offered to jump on a plane immediately to be with her. But in Linda fashion, she said to not rush home, that it was just a bump in the road and that she would be all better and ready for the annual beach trip to Ocean City, Maryland, in July. Linda was strong physically, mentally, and in her faith—so we had no doubt that by the summer, everything would be back to normal.

Through every chemo session, every surgery, every good day, every bad day—Linda was fueled to fight by her "later." She fought for our wedding, she fought for her retirement, she fought for her future grandchildren, the family vacations—she fought for all of the moments she knew she had ahead of her. As time went on and her cancer got more and more aggressive, it *never* stopped her from fighting for her "later."

Linda got through three rounds of chemotherapy and a full hysterectomy. After surgery, we were told that the chemo wasn't as successful as they hoped for, and that the cancer was growing and spreading. Still, Linda never lost faith. A few weeks into her recovery, she was experiencing some complications and was admitted to the hospital. The night she was admitted happened to be the night of Best Life Live. Nick didn't tell me about what was going on until after I got off stage, and as always—he was cool, calm, and collected as he told me. Clearly, he got that from Linda.

Even during her time in the hospital—she was always FaceTiming us, talking about how eager she was to get strong enough to go home and knock out the next round of chemo. All she wanted to do was to go home—and she had her heart, mind, and strength set on it.

It was Monday, June 3, and Linda was still in the hospital. Nick was flying home from a business trip in Toronto, and I was flying home from visiting my family in Michigan. Somehow, that Monday, we both ended up having a layover in Atlanta and were on the same flight back to Austin. I landed in Atlanta about an hour later than Nick. As soon as my plane landed, I was antsy to rush off the plane and find him at our gate. I hated being away from him, especially with everything that was going on.

I sprinted to gate B9, giddy to be reunited with my fiancé. When I saw him though, I knew something was wrong— without him saying a single word. I walked up to him with panic in my heart, gave him a hug, and waited for what I had a feeling was bad news.

"My mom's in the ICU," he said. "Things took a turn and she's having trouble breathing on her own, so they had to intubate her. My dad has a meeting with the doctors in an hour to talk about life expectancy."

Life expectancy? That can't be right. We were supposed to be going to Pennsylvania in a couple of days to be there and help out around the house when she was *discharged* from the hospital. The panic that was in my heart rushed to the rest of my body. Even with all of the hustle and chaos surrounding us in the terminal, I could hear my heart beating out of my chest. We got called to board the plane and my stomach immediately dropped because I remembered that our seats weren't together. I asked him if he wanted me to try and switch with the person sitting next to him, and he told me to not go through the trouble for such a short flight. I may have been three rows behind him during that flight back to Austin, but it felt like I was across the world from him. I just wanted to hold his hand. I just wanted to talk to him. Knowing that Nick's dad was having the meeting with the doctors while we were flying made the flight back to Austin the longest two-hour flight of our lives.

We landed in Austin and Nick hadn't heard from his dad

yet. So we got our bags and headed home. We drove separately to the airport because we flew out at different times, so I got in my car and went straight to the dog sitter to pick up our pup while Nick drove straight home. I drove in silence waiting for my phone to ring, but it never did. As soon as I got home, I walked into our house through the garage, which opens up into our laundry/mudroom. Nick had only been home for about a half hour, and I noticed that the washer was running. My heart sunk. Nick *never* does laundry this quickly after returning home from a trip. In fact, his packed suitcase normally sits in our closet for at least a week after a trip. I quickly put two and two together. The only reason Nick would be doing laundry this quickly after a trip is if he had to leave again. I knew that he must have talked to his dad and gotten news that meant he had to get to Pennsylvania as soon as possible. I walked back into the house and immediately noticed that Nick's face was flushed. I was terrified to hear what he had to say.

"So I talked to my dad. They gave her a week."

It was the kind of moment that leaves a forever scar on your heart. It was something I had only ever seen in movies or soap operas before, and somehow it had become our reality. With tears in his eyes, Nick told me that he and his brother were taking the first flight home the next morning. *A week?* Things took a turn so quickly and none of us had anticipated being told we had such little time left with her. As I hugged my fiancé, I could feel his heart breaking. The worst part was, I couldn't do anything to put it back together.

Nick and his brother left for Pennsylvania the next morning, while I stayed back in Texas for a couple of days so that the boys could spend some alone time with their mother. Saying goodbye to him that morning was the absolute hardest thing I've ever had to do. All I wanted to do was jump on that plane holding his hand the entire way, but I knew that I had to let him go. The two days in Texas I had by myself were two of the most challenging days I've ever faced, but I knew it was nothing compared to what Nick was going through. I felt like half of my heart was missing—and the half that I did have, was breaking for the love of my life. This wasn't supposed to happen. It wasn't a part of our plan. But in life, I've learned that there really is no such thing as a plan.

I arrived in Pennsylvania late that Thursday night, beyond eager to be reunited with Nick. That night, I remember crawling into bed next to my emotionally and physically exhausted fiancé, holding him tighter than I ever had before. In that moment, I was so grateful that we had found each other before all of this—it happened this way for a reason.

First thing the next morning, we made our way to the

hospital to visit Linda. I don't think I had ever been more nervous than I was in the moment we stepped onto the ICU floor. I took a few deep breaths and gave myself a mental pep talk to force myself to hold it together. When I felt the tears coming up, I reminded myself to be as strong as Linda. I took one last deep breath and made my way to Linda's room. Before entering the room, we had to put on gloves and a sanitary mask. While I was tying my mask in the doorway, I caught a glimpse of our sweet Linda sitting up in her bed. She still had her ventilator in, but the look in her eyes the moment she saw me in the doorway was one that I will never forget. I instantly felt her warmth and all of my nerves went away—just like the very first time I met her.

We entered the room and I walked over to squeeze her hand. She immediately started writing on her mini dry erase board, which was the only way she could communicate with the ventilator in. She flipped the dry erase board over, and it read "Welcome!!!" I laughed. She *would* be welcoming me into her own hospital room. I told her how happy I was to see her, and how jealous I was of her fresh, pink manicure and pedicure. She told me the nurses did it for her.

Still in shock, I didn't know the right thing to say. The minute silence filled the air, she started scribbling on her dry erase board again. This time, it read: "You two need to talk because I can't. I'll just listen!" Linda never *was* really good at silence—she always had a story to tell, a compliment to give, or a laugh to let out. So that's what we did, we talked.

A few hours later, while Nick and I were in the waiting room while she had other visitors, we were told that Linda was finally going to get her ventilator taken out, after a long four days. We rushed back to her room, excited and eager to finally hear her voice again. We coached her through the entire process and she by no surprise handled it like a warrior. After the ventilator was out and the doctor asked her to say her name as loud as she could, the first words she said to us were, "I love you." Tears were rolling down our faces as she went on and on to tell us about all of the things she had been thinking about over the past four days. She told us that she loved us and that she was going to fight. She told us that she was going to live forever and couldn't wait to be the best grandma ever one day. It was a moment that I will never forget.

After the ventilator was out, Linda's spirits were high and focused on fighting. Her energy and strength made us believe that she had a chance of pulling off a miracle. If anyone could pull off a miracle, it was Linda.

A few hours later, we had a meeting with the doctor. After evaluating her condition, the doctor told us that the cancer had grown into a beast. All of the nutrients that they were giving Linda were just fueling the cancer, making it more and more aggressive. We were told that with the rate at which the cancer was growing, there was nothing else they could do. The plan was to get Linda home the next day and have in-home Hospice care to make her as comfortable as possible. But Linda had other plans. She kept insisting that she had to go home *that* day, which was Friday. We didn't think it was possible due to the fact that she had only been off the ventilator for a few hours. But somehow, she convinced the doctors, the stars aligned, and after a long three weeks in the hospital—Linda was finally going home.

One of the first things Linda said to Nick after the meeting with the doctor was that she was going to miss our wedding. It was one of our greatest fears, one that we never thought would become a reality. But we weren't going to let that happen. In an emotional waiting room conversation, Nick and I decided to have a ceremony the next day at their house so that Linda could be a part of our wedding. As we walked back into her room to tell her the news, we squeezed her hands as tears filled our eyes. The beautiful, tragic moment we told her about the wedding ceremony was another that I will never forget.

While the word "Hospice" scared us all, Linda was going home with full intentions to keep fighting the fight. She knew that her body was fighting against her, but that didn't put the slightest dent in her faith. When we got her home that Friday night, her spirits were up but her energy was low. We told her to try and rest as much as she could, because she had a wedding to attend the next day!

Saturday was a special day, for many reasons. The sun was shining and she was home, constantly surrounded by all of her friends and family. She was exhausted, but you would have never known it by the constant smile that was across her face. Linda was basically a celebrity in their Central Pennsylvania small town, which meant a lot of friends, family, and community members wanted to see her. She didn't turn down a single person. Saturday morning was filled with storytelling, reminiscing through old photos, tears, laughter, hugs, foot rubs, hand squeezes, and indescribable amounts of love. Between visitors, when the house would quiet down a bit, reality sunk in. I was overwhelmed by her positivity and strength despite the circumstance. I didn't understand how she could do it. It just didn't feel real.

When 2 o'clock rolled around, it was time to get ready for the "wedding"—I put wedding in quotes because it wasn't an official ceremony due to the fact that we didn't have time to get a marriage license, but that didn't change a thing in our eyes, or Linda's. I needed my future mother-in-law to be present on the day that her son said "I do." I wanted to make the promises to her that I had planned on making to her on May 9, 2020, which was our wedding date. I wanted to promise her that I would take care of her son, love him fiercely no matter what, and be the best wife, mother, and daughter-in-law that I could possibly be.

I wore a casual white dress that I had found at a local mall the day before. We got Nick a ring from a local jeweler, along with a new shirt and tie. We even picked out a dress, jewelry, and matching ball cap to dress Linda in so that she could feel her absolute best for the ceremony. She looked more radiant and stunning than ever. Their family pastor arrived at their house, and it was time to get married.

At 3 p.m. on Saturday, June 8, 2019—I stood in front of a recliner where my future mother-in-law was fighting for her life and said "I do" to the love of my life in the living room of his childhood home. It wasn't a part of our plan. It wasn't the way we "pictured" it, it wasn't the way things should have been, but it was absolutely *perfect*, because she was there.

After the ceremony ended, we were about to make a toast when Linda asked us all to gather around her even closer. She then went on to give about a ten-minute speech that ended up being the most emotional, life-changing ten minutes of my life. She told us all how much she loved us, how much she would miss us, how sad she felt that she was going to miss out on so much—but how excited she was to be reunited with her mother, father, and sister-in-law who passed away just a few months earlier from cancer. She ended her speech by telling us that if we ever wanted to see her again, we had to believe in Him and be a follower of Christ. There wasn't a dry eye in the house.

It was one of those moments that changes everything. There was life before Linda's speech, and now there's life after her speech. It changed us, it strengthened us, and it made us realize how short life really is.

On the morning of Monday, June 10, 2019, Linda became an angel and was sent to heaven. Her battle with cancer came to an end, and she was finally pain-free. We couldn't help but realize the crazy timing of it all, thinking back to when Linda demanded that she go home on Friday night. If she hadn't pushed to go home that night, we wouldn't have been blessed with the amazing day we had with her on Saturday. We truly believe that she knew and trusted God's timing of it all.

I learned more in the last days we had with Linda than I had in my entire twenty-seven years of life. When you go through something like that, all of the little things in life completely disappear. They instantly don't matter. All

that matters are the people in life that you love uncon-
ditionally—and the ones who love you back *just* as hard.
As I held my fiancé's hand as he lost his mother, the
first woman he ever loved, I realized that when you lose
someone you love—life is over. I know that sounds earth-
shattering and dramatic, but it's true. Life as you *knew* it
was over. You have to start over. You have to learn to live
without someone you never wanted to live without. I was
so grateful for the fact that Nick and I found each other
before all of this, and I knew it happened for a reason. I
knew that we went through such a difficult time during
our engagement for a *reason*. I may not understand the
reason, but I understand the lessons that it taught me.

That's why I chose to share this story with you. I did it so
I could share the biggest, most important lesson that I
have *ever* learned—and that lesson is that your "later" is
not guaranteed. This chapter may have been the most
difficult to write and yes, it may have taken me triple the
amount of time to write as the others did, but I did it so
that you won't spend one more *second* of your life without
understanding how precious it really is.

One of the biggest things I learned about Linda in the
time that I was blessed to have with her was that she never
lived her life waiting for later. She lived every single day
filled to the brim with love, laughter, and faith—she woke
up every single morning with passion and purpose and a

fire in her heart that warmed each and every person she encountered. She lived more in her fifty-seven years of life than most of us would in one-hundred. *That's* how you show up. *That's* how you live your life.

You know that dream we keep talking about, the one that's been locked in your heart? The one that you want to set free, but you just keep telling yourself that you'll do it *later*? The one that you say you'll do when you're ready, when the time is right, when you lose the weight, or when you have the help. Yes, *that* dream. The one you keep putting off. You need to pursue it *now*. Don't waste one more second of this life that you have been blessed with, because no matter how hard we try to control or plan our lives, none of that is up to us. That's not *our* job. The only job we have is to show up every single day, living out our purpose. If you don't wake up every single day with your purpose *pouring* out of your heart, you aren't doing it right. Girl, take this as your final wake-up call. If I could reach out of this book and shake you with my own two arms, I would. Life is too short. *Stop* living your life for later. Live it like Linda did.

Conclusion

Alright girl, take a deep breath. You *did* it. I told you that this wasn't going to be a piece of cake, didn't I? Like I said in the very beginning of this book, I may not know your name or what your dream is—but if you picked up this book and got to this point, I *do* know this about you: the next version of you is *ready* to be unveiled.

This book is no magic pill. It didn't make all of your inse-curities, excuses, and doubts vanish into thin air. I'm no Oprah, remember? Those insecurities, excuses, and doubts are still there, and that's okay. I have days when mine are still there, too. But now, you have the tools that will help you put in the work to push past them. Your pur-pose is clearer than ever. You realize that you are not the only one who's felt this way. The fire in your heart that had been slowly fading or put out completely is *back* and it's stronger, brighter and fiercer than ever. But it's *your* job to not let it burn out again.

As much as I would love for you to pass this book along to your friend, your mother, your sister, your roommate, your coworker, or the random girl you spark a conversation with in the bathroom at the bar, I want *you* to hold onto it. This is yours. I want you to come back to it on days when you feel that fire trying to put itself out again. Because there *will* be those kinds of days. There will be days when all of this seems like bullshit and all of this seems impossible all over again. But that's what this book is for—so that you can come back to it. So that you can remind yourself that *you got this.* This book is to remind you that your purpose is way stronger than your insecurities.

Remember that you are working on you, *for* you. You aren't doing this for your partner, your parents, your siblings, your friends, your boss, or your social media followers. You are doing this for *you.* And if you are really going to do this for you, that means you have to learn to say no. You have to learn to say it without feeling guilty. Remember that setting boundaries is healthy and it's an absolute necessity when it comes to respecting and taking care of yourself and your dream. If something is not serving you and the life you want to create for yourself, it's time to walk away in peace. You are not setting boundaries and saying no to disappoint or offend people. You are doing it to manage the priorities and goals you have set for your life.

You may have reached the end of this book, but girl, this is just the beginning. I've been there—I've been on the last page of an inspiring self-help book and felt ready to conquer the world. But then I closed the book, and I didn't *change* anything—so, nothing changed. I stayed stuck. Please, learn from my mistakes. Don't close this book without making or planning your first change. It can be small, but you have to do it. You didn't come this far, to only come *this* far. And that's the thing about personal growth—it's going to feel like you are never making progress. It's going to feel like your dream is slowly inching further and further *away* from you. You'll have days when you feel like you are stuck in reverse or just plain stuck. But then one day—out of *freaking* nowhere, you'll do something that will make you realize you have become the next you. She's waiting for you; now, go get her.

About the Author

STEFANY BANDA has built an online community of like-minded women by creating inspiring, relatable content that she shares through YouTube videos, social media, blog posts, and motivational live events. After graduating from college, Stefany went straight into the 9-5 corporate life. She quickly realized that spending forty hours a week in a roller chair working for someone else's dream was not for her. Down-to-earth and driven to always keep it real with her audience, she makes it a priority to show the parts of life that most of us hide outside of social media's "highlight reel." To connect with Stefany, visit StefanyBanda.com.